# ENTWINED

ANGELA SAUSMAN

**BALBOA.**PRESS

A DIVISION OF HAY HOUSE

Balboa Press books may be ordered through booksellers or by contacting:

Balboa Press
A Division of Hay House
1663 Liberty Drive
Bloomington, IN 47403
www.balboapress.com.au
AU TFN: 1 800 844 925 (Toll Free inside Australia)
AU Local: 0283 107 086 (+61 2 8310 7086 from outside Australia)

Because of the dynamic nature of the Internet, any web addresses or links contained in this book may have changed since publication and may no longer be valid. The views expressed in this work are solely those of the author and do not necessarily reflect the views of the publisher, and the publisher hereby disclaims any responsibility for them.

The author of this book does not dispense medical advice or prescribe the use of any technique as a form of treatment for physical, emotional, or medical problems without the advice of a physician, either directly or indirectly. The intent of the author is only to offer information of a general nature to help you in your quest for emotional and spiritual well-being. In the event you use any of the information in this book for yourself, which is your constitutional right, the author and the publisher assume no responsibility for your actions.

Print information available on the last page.

ISBN: 978-1-5043-1932-4 (sc)
ISBN: 978-1-5043-1933-1 (e)

Balboa Press rev. date: 12/09/2020

# INTRODUCTION

If you are reading this, chances are you are about to embark on or have ventured onto the roller-coaster ride of horse ownership, making a dream come true; but are you ready?

Horses, (I will use this term to refer to both horses and ponies) are amazing, intelligent, sentient beings. If you are already a horse addict like me you will understand the overwhelming need to be with an equine companion: you find their smell intoxicating, their touch revitalising and their company fulfilling. All these attributes can inoculate you against the trials and tribulations of horse ownership.

However, if you are entering the horse world with the innocence of an equine voyeur or caving in from the incessant pleading of a loved one, the first step in turning the 'dream' into reality should be to understand a little about the horse's world and, just as importantly, how it will affect your own!

Preparing for horse ownership is more than a check sheet or an equine shopping list; equine-centric horse ownership is a selflessness like no other. My horses eat before I do, have a much larger shoe budget, and have far more massages and spa experiences than I do, all in return for a laughingly undemanding work contract. However, I love them and my way of life, and I put their welfare first—they are my responsibility and one that I take very seriously. That's only fair, our relationship was of my choosing, not theirs!

It has taken a few decades of learning from some amazing horsemen and horsewomen for me to understand the holistic relationship between the human/equine mind and body, how each facet can work in sync, and how to interpret the environmental effects and their consequences—and all the while learning how each scenario has a domino, knock-on effect.

I have chosen to concentrate on a selection of these teachings and have categorised them into six chapters. I will be taking a brief look at both the human and equine mind and body, exploring many of the environmental influences and offering a practical look at the gear and equipment that is needed and why.

Preparing for and managing a horse's needs, making the right choices, can be daunting but awareness is the starting point.

This is where the concept of *Entwined* began.

# ACKNOWLEDGEMENTS

A heartfelt thank you to all the many horsemen and horsewomen who have helped develop my understanding of the horse world. From sharing your knowledge and experiences *Entwined* evolved.

Tanja Mitton, Georgia Bruce, Dr Andrew Easton, BVScMACVSc (Veterinary Dentistry) CMAVA, Sarah Tomlinson for your professional help—your input has been enlightening and invaluable.

My friend and coach, Kim Weston—thank you for your tireless patience and encouragement, Kim.

My father, John Hutt—living with a horse addict is not an easy undertaking. I truly appreciate the many days, mostly in inclement UK weather conditions, when you waited patiently for me to finish my horse fix. Thanks, Dad.

My husband, Michael—for all you do for me and the horses—we love you!

Finally, thank you to Spritz, APH Swish, Cristogracia Dantes and Don Versprechen, my horses—their wonderful personalities brighten every day.

# INFLUENCES ON YOUR HORSE LIFESTYLE

There are two major factors that influence how your horse fits into your lifestyle: **time** and **money**, both of which need considerable thought and planning.

## Time

It has been said many times in the equine world that becoming involved with horses is the biggest time-waster! It is easy to let caring for a horse swallow up the hours in the day. I would recommend spending a few moments to make a time budget. If you already own a horse, start by taking a fresh look at the time spent with your horse.

If you are looking at this aspect for the first time or need a little help analysing what you already do, you can go to the *Entwined* toolkit at oceaneasy.net and select the time budget tool.

This includes:

- **Travel time to the yard**
- **Feeding**
- **Watering**
- **Paddock management**
- **Wellness checks**
- **Grooming**
- **Riding for pleasure**

- Vet/farrier visits
- Training/clinics
- Feed/forage collection/ deliveries
- Competitions

Once completed ask yourself:

- **Can you dedicate enough time to your horse for their comfort and wellbeing?**
- **Do you have a horse/work/family/friends/fun balance?**
- **Can you allocate enough time to achieve your horsey goals?**

## Money

There are many different needs to be considered when budgeting for a horse. Breaking this down to a monthly analysis can help plan for the everyday expenses and the unexpected. Reading through the chapters 'The Horse's Surroundings' and 'Gear and Equipment Explained' will help in compiling a list of 'must-haves'.

There is a money budget tool available in the *Entwined* toolkit at oceaneasy. net to help with planning. Be aware there is no such thing as a cheap horse! The money budget planner takes into consideration the following:

- **Veterinary care**
- **Feed**
- **Grooming equipment**
- **Horse wear (rugs, boots etc.)**
- **Saddlery and tack**
- **Training**
- **Agistment/livery/boarding**
- **Paddock/stabling maintenance**
- **Riding wear**
- **Shows and competitions**
- **Transport**
- **Memberships and insurance**

There are of course many further influencing factors within an individual's lifestyle that may need to be considered before making the decision to leap into horse ownership and these should be examined by the same methodical process.

# HOW THE HUMAN MIND WORKS

## How we think, react, feel and learn

I know you want to delve into the horse's world but it really does begin with you!

Let's start with two questions:

How open-minded are you?

Do we use 10 per cent of our brain or all of it?

In the past, it was suggested that we use just 10 per cent of our brain, a medical theory which arose after people sustained brain injuries yet were still able to function. However, modern science has now changed our view on the 10 per cent rule by proving, through evidence-based research, that we use all our brain's capacity at different times for different tasks. What was once a theory based on a logical thought process has been shown to be incorrect through the use of MRI images or PET scans.

That's all very well but how does this relate to our thinking in the horse world?

The point is, we need to be open-minded and realise that the old ways may not be the best ways: be aware that the horse world is steeped in tradition and history. Yes, there are 'masters', the many horsemen and horsewomen who have a wealth of knowledge and who inspire us, but in the modern horse world I would encourage the use of critical thinking in a positive way. How many people question everything they do, both for and with their horses? It takes practice to build this mindset, but the rewards are worth it. An inquisitive mind, an incentive to research the latest thinking or innovations, will ultimately offer the ability to make more informed decisions for a better outcome. That could take many forms: a better understanding, a happier owner, a more comfortable environment for the horse, a saving in time or money.

**Let's get technical!**

In simple terms the human brain is the body's command centre, sending messages to the body through a network of connecting wires (motor neurons and nerves) and receiving messages from the whole body and the surrounding environment. This network is called the nervous system and is responsible for controlling how we think, react, feel and learn.

**How we think about our horses**

There are many different relationships we can have with our horses; it is a good idea to examine how a horse fits, or would fit, into your lifestyle. Are they an animate piece of sports equipment, a companion, a work tool or a pet/family member?

You'll probably find that you can relate to one, more or even all these scenarios, but in each role, they remain horses and this fact needs to be respected: their needs met as well as our own wants satisfied.

Of course, there is no right or wrong answer on how someone should perceive their relationship with a horse, but being aware of that can help in the process of making informed decisions, while keeping the horse's welfare and our emotions in check (a little more on those topics in a moment).

**How we react**

Our reaction times are much slower than those of horses; this has consequences for our safety around horses as well as impacting on handling, riding and training. Even though we have brought horses into our domestic world they are still prey creatures with a huge difference in sensitivity to the environment from our own. They need to be quick to stay alive!

If, while interacting with our horses, we can increase awareness and react correctly but faster, it will help to manage or control situations. This can be invaluable in avoiding injury, as well as improving ability both in the saddle and on the ground with handling, riding and training horses.

Raising your awareness is the key here: knowing the proximity of our bodies in relation to that of the horse's, understanding how and when horses are likely to react to their surroundings by reading their body language and the warning signals is definitely an undertaking that is worth the effort.

It is possible to train our reaction times to stimuli and to improve timing with repetition and practice. To get a good indication of your own reaction time, hold the bottom of a ruler in your fingertips, let it go and catch it again, noting at which mark you successfully stopped the ruler falling. With planning, repetition and practice the task should become quicker, the measurement less and less. Think about what actions you need to release and catch the ruler. Repeat these actions and keep practicing to improve your reaction times.

This process—planning, repetition and practice—is the same for any task you wish to master.

So, for instance, when picking out a horse's hoof, apart from the correct body positioning and procedure to correctly handle your horse to perform the task, you need to also think about (plan) your actions to swiftly and quietly move out of the way if the horse is startled. So, be aware of your surroundings, plan the action and build on the ability to use quick reactions to avoid injury and control the situation.

## How we feel and control emotions

Awareness of feelings and emotions (known as emotional intelligence in the management field), relates to a level of understanding and control of emotional reactions.

To be an effective handler, rider and trainer of a horse, emotions need to be kept in check. Realising that human feelings directly affect horses' reactions is the first step and then understanding how horses think (a basic overview is given in the next chapter 'How the Horse's Mind Works') is imperative to responding correctly. There are many diverse scenarios that provoke emotional reactions in handlers, riders and trainers but knowledge of a horse's cognitive ability and behaviour will help with correct responses. To learn the discipline of responding in an informed and considered manner involves learning to stop, think and then act appropriately. This, of course, can be easier said than done, especially because a horse reacts to environmental stimuli faster than we do; it takes repetition and practice to act in a considered manner in all the diverse horse situations you will find yourself in. In fact, the same process of planning (to stop and think) followed by action with repetition and practice, is relevant in controlling emotional as well as physical reactions.

Our thoughts affect our body through the brain's release of chemical signals, resulting in electrical energy that transmits impulses to nerve and muscle cells. Horses read (or learn to read) the resulting human body language that is created and respond accordingly. A person who appears calm and confident will have a mirroring effect on the horse's behaviour. Conversely a person who is a bag of nerves will result in the horse looking out for what has caused the nervousness. Where is that tiger?

There have been many times that I have felt like a swan around horses, looking calm and serene but paddling furiously beneath the surface. It can fool the horse for a moment, but they can and will pick up on the chemical and nervous energy. Controlling your inner calm is imperative for a harmonious relationship!

## Understanding the human mind

There are tools available to assist with concentration, learning, memory and decision making, but in the horse world, neuro-linguistic programming (NLP) is popular with riders and handlers at all levels of experience to examine how their minds affect their handling, riding and training of horses.

NLP Master Coach *Tanja Mitton explains:

> NLP is a hybrid science discovered and then further developed in the late 1960s by computer scientist Richard Bandler and linguist John Grinder.
>
> It is a powerful body of information about how the human mind works, which has been further built up since the 1970s and continues to evolve through new research. The way we think (neuro) and communicate (linguistic) affects both behaviour and emotions.
>
> Being aware of your mindset is a key factor in the horse world; from taking that first trail ride to riding in high-level competitions, mindset coaching is a valuable resource. It can help individuals understand how their mind works and offer tools and strategies to help achieve goals and ambitions.

### An exciting new development

The fact that how someone thinks affects their relationship, ride and performance with their horse is scientifically proven, but this information has been haphazardly delivered in the past without a logical sequence for handlers, riders and trainers to build on.

Tanja has recently clarified this pathway in the form of a training scale for the rider or trainer to follow, helping them to achieve objectives with their chosen horse.

There are three parts to Tanja's training scale (Mindset, The Rider, and The Horse). Here is a snippet from Tanja's book *It Takes Two to Tango* detailing the first rung of the Mindset Training Scale 'Overcoming Limiting Beliefs':

> Limiting beliefs often start when we are very young and are shaped by what other people say to us and the experiences we have while growing up. Our environment and the people around us play a big role in how we see ourselves and the beliefs we take on. Often limiting beliefs are pure illusion and have no relevance to reality, however by identifying with them and focusing on them we make them part of our reality. Most people end up living their entire lives holding onto their limiting beliefs and taking action according to what they believe they can or can't do.
>
> Common limiting beliefs are:
>
> • **I am not good enough**
>     I.   **To succeed at a certain level**
>     II.  **To make a team selection**
>     III. **To be someone special**
>
> • **I am not worthy**
>     I.   **To be noticed**
>     II.  **To associate with riders who are better than me**
>     III. **To have a good horse and own nice gear**
>
> • **Lack of finance**
>     I.   **I'll never be successful because I can't afford an expensive horse**
>     II.  **You need money to be a professional rider**
>     III. **Even when you work hard you only just have enough money**

- **Always unlucky**
  - I. **I am always the unlucky one**
  - II. **No matter how hard I try good things never happen to me**
  - III. **Whenever things are going well it is only a matter of time before everything falls apart again**

We all have an image of ourselves that details who we are, what we can and can't do, our talents and abilities, our faults and limitations. These images become the road map of our actions, which in turn determines our behaviour, what we say and how we react to our day-to-day experiences. Most people find it easier to see qualities in others rather than themselves and therefore we tend to encourage other people around us much more then we encourage ourselves.

## How we learn

We all travel through life learning as we go, most of the time stumbling through situations where we were expected to learn skills or information. Sometimes this worked and sometimes not. I have certainly been in situations where my preferred style of learning and the information delivery were at odds with each other. To explain this further here are the three main learning modalities that relate to riding:

- **Visual, learning through sight, e.g. books, videos, demonstration**
- **Kinaesthetic, learning by doing, e.g. riding, feeling, experimenting**
- **Auditory, learning by listening, e.g. instruction, direction, music**

These main modalities can be broken down further into eight recognised styles of learning:

- **Visual (spatial)**
  - Pictures, images and spatial understanding
- **Verbal (linguistic)**
  - Words, both speech and writing
- **Kinaesthetic (physical)**
  - Feeling with both the body and hands, a sense of touch
- **Auditory (aural, musical)**
  - Sound and music
- **Solitary (intrapersonal)**
  - Studying alone
- **Social (interpersonal)**
  - Study with others—groups
- **Logical (mathematical)**
  - Logic—reasoning and systems
- **Naturalistic**
  - Scientific reasoning

**Identifying your learning style**

Everyone will have a preferred learning style (or, more likely, a combination of styles) and in turn each style has benefits and drawbacks in any given situation.

These eight learning styles can be used at different times to enhance a way of learning; understanding and selecting a preferred learning style can make learning less stressful and more rewarding.

**Information delivery**

Understanding and analysing how we learn in the horse world is simple. This is done by examining how the information is delivered.

Information can be given in the following ways:

- **Listening to a presenter/instructor/coach/parent/friend**
- **Watching videos/presentations**
- **Riding by feel**
- **Viewing rider position/horse positioning in a mirror**
- **Attending lessons/clinics/workshops**
- **Viewing diagrams and images**
- **Reading books/magazines**
- **Visiting websites and searching social media**
- **Phone coaching**
- **Realtime virtual coaching**

This is where positive critical thinking can help. If, for example, an individual prefers to learn by watching (visual, spatial) but they are mostly learning about horses and themselves through an instructor who gives verbal instructions (verbal, linguistic), maybe it's time to make a change or take another approach to their training.

That doesn't mean that they need to stop what they are currently doing but maybe modify to help themselves learn more easily. So, in this example, as they prefer to learn by watching, arranging for someone to video their lesson so that they can take a fresh look at it later will enhance their learning.

It has taken years for me to be brave enough to politely decline a group learning experience or to avoid shouty instructions (and not just in the horse world!). I know now that I learn more quickly on a one-to-one basis, often followed by taking further time alone to work on the information for the best result. Being shouted at just results in my becoming flustered. Take time to analyse what works for you.

## The problem of groupthink

Reading this far has hopefully already encouraged a little critical thinking. In many situations we find ourselves, it often seems safer to go with the crowd and not challenge the common belief (something we call groupthink); but is this in the best interests of the individual or the horse? Some may feel more comfortable learning alone rather than in a crowd (like myself). While it is often easier to apply critical thinking in a solitary environment, here are a few suggestions to help with critical thinking when in a group situation:

- **Use of active listening (really listen to what people are saying) and gain as much information as possible**
- **Be prepared to politely question the professional, tutor or peers if a better understanding of a topic is needed**
- **If still undecided on whether the right answer has been reached (for human and horse), then research alternative options but keep an open-mind**
- **Reach a conclusion and not a judgement; remember everyone is different, both humans and horses**

## Learning the right thing

In today's world words like 'expert' and 'professional' seem to have become commonplace, a little like the 'executive' in 'executive home'. There can be some confusion as to how someone becomes an expert. I would start with suggesting that it is a label that is awarded not self-proclaimed.

The same goes for expert information in the horse world. The internet is a double-edged sword where this is concerned. We have access to far more information than the local library can offer but what to believe?

## Research

There are many ways that you can find information, but the information needs to be:

- **High quality and credible**
- **Current and timely**
- **Beneficial to you**
- **Beneficial to your chosen horse**
- **Correct for you and your chosen horse at a point in time**

Is it high quality and credible?

- **Where has the information come from?**
- **Who has researched it?**
- **Was the research evidence based or from logical thought?**
- **Was it peer reviewed?**
- **Who paid for the research and were there vested interests involved?**

Is it current and timely?

- **How long has this theory/method been available?**
- **Is there any more up-to-date thinking on the topic that needs to be considered?**

Is this beneficial for you?

- **Does it fit with your learning style?**
- **Is it practical to add to or change your management or training system you have already adopted?**

Is this beneficial for my chosen horse?

- **As each horse is different, is this the best option or training method for your horse?**
- **What are the alternative options?**

Is this correct for you and your chosen horse at this moment in time?

- **Does it fit with your current skill level?**
- **Does it fit with your horse's current level of training?**

There should now be a better understanding of how to examine your mind and how to select information to enhance your learning and help you make informed decisions. Of course, there is always trial and error, but analyse and learn from your mistakes.

# HOW THE HORSE'S MIND WORKS

## Behaviour, learning and communication

Horse behaviour is a fascinating subject and to have the best relationship and achieve the best performance from any horse, a basic understanding of how their minds work is needed.

### The horse's hardwiring

How and where a horse is kept can differ greatly from their evolutionary environment and being mindful of any differences will lead to a better understanding of how they are adapting to their current lifestyle.

There are horses that still roam their native environments, such as the Dartmoor Pony in southwest England. Horses in such a natural environment may roam freely over vast areas of pasture land; they can cover up to 26 kilometres in 24 hours while grazing usually for between 16 to 20 hours of that time. The distance travelled and the amount of grazing time is mostly determined by the quality of grazing available. Rarely does the space and quality of grazing provided by a domestic setting match this natural state.

There is more information on changes from the evolutionary environment to the domestic setting in the chapter 'The Horse's Surroundings', for now, think of the horse's mind as being programmed to satisfy their natural grazing needs. In fact, I often refer to our horses as large eating machines on legs!

## The prey animal

Humans and horses have a long history, and while man has practised selective breeding for desirable traits, (equine) evolution usually works on much longer time frames; the horse remains a prey animal with natural instincts for fight or flight.

## Let's get technical!

When a horse believes it is in danger, the amygdala within their brain is stimulated. The stimulus creates activity along the sympathetic-adrenal-medullary axis (SAM) which triggers a physiological response—production of the blood hormone, adrenaline. A horse now has the energy boost they need to fight the danger or run. The fight response in a horse translates to kicking or biting, and the flight response to shying or bolting.

### How the horse controls their response

The SAM process is immediate, faster than we can comprehend, so how can you train a horse not to fight or run when they see something new that they are unsure of? Luckily, there is a second, much slower process that is activated within the hippocampus, a part of the horse's brain next to the amygdala. This reaction is along the hypothalamic-pituitary-adrenal axis (HPA), the part of the brain which is responsible for cognitive processes—basically where a horse evaluates and learns. With patience and repetition, it is possible to train a horse to cope in situations where their initial reaction may be one of fight or flight.

### The horse's reaction to pain

Horses and other prey animals have the ability to mask chemical signals triggered by their brain, disguising reactions to pain. In situations of perceived danger, a horse may suppress their pain which would normally lead to fight or flight, a condition called stress-induced analgesia. This fact should never be forgotten. If everyday handling, riding and training are done sympathetically and with empathy, this condition should not arise, but it pays to remember that just because everything looks OK, doesn't mean it is OK!

## How the horse learns

The horse's mind is fully functioning at birth as with all prey animals; these are known as precocial species. They learn quickly and never forget!

Equine learning theory is a broad and fascinating subject. Internationally renowned animal behaviourist *Georgia Bruce explains that there are three main ways in which horses learn:

1. **Habituation** (broadly speaking **desensitisation**): e.g. becoming used to flags blowing in the breeze at a show ring.

   Includes the following methods:

   **Counter-conditioning, systematic desensitisation, approach-and-retreat, flooding, and over-shadowing.**

   Desensitising a horse to factors in their environment takes time. Seek expert advice on the most appropriate method to use for the situation in hand.

2. **Classical conditioning** (a subconscious linking of a previously meaningless stimulus with a meaningful stimulus): e.g. the noise of feed buckets being prepared and linking this sound with food.

3. **Operant conditioning** (trial and error learning). It is about a behaviour and consequences. If a behaviour is immediately followed by reinforcement it will occur

more often. If it is followed by punishment it will occur less often.

- **Positive reinforcement:** e.g. a treat for horses that are motivated by food rewards
- **Negative reinforcement:** e.g. leg aid pressure being taken away as a reward
- **Positive punishment:** e.g. the shock of an electric fence
- **Negative punishment:** e.g. yard confinement in response to disrespect of fencing
- **Extinction:** is a fifth element of operant conditioning. A behaviour that previously was reinforced may gradually decrease if it is no longer followed by reinforcement. The behaviour may first go through an 'extinction burst' (last ditch extreme effort) before the horse gives up on the behaviour all together. Extinction protocol is a powerful and ethical way to reduce or eliminate undesirable behaviour without punishment

Every time a human interacts with a horse, they are either teaching the horse to behave in a certain way or reinforcing a previously learned behaviour, whether intentional or not.

A good example of this is when a horse thinks it's a great idea to use a conveniently placed human shoulder to satisfy the need to scratch an itchy nose. Allowing that to happen when the situation is seen as 'acceptable' (when an old T-shirt is worn while completing horsey chores) reinforces the behaviour; surprise, surprise the same behaviour will happen when the white competition shirt is worn on that convenient shoulder. The behaviour has already been reinforced as OK, so why should the rider become upset when their pristine white competition shirt is covered in goo? The horse can't be expected to know that is totally 'unacceptable'? To the horse the scenario is exactly the same, itchy nose—convenient shoulder!

This constitutes human error, not horse error; always be mindful of the behaviours you are reinforcing!

In horse training and equine learning, it has been scientifically proven that reward-based training is a faster means to achieve the behaviour required, whether the horse is learning to stand still to be groomed or learning to perform a particular movement. The reward-based system is the way to go.

This is an excellent example of science reinforcing logical reasoning, it stands to reason that if a horse is learning in a relaxed positive environment the outcome will be pleasing for both horse and human.

**Boredom and unwanted vices**

Horses in their evolutionary habitat are mentally stimulated by their environment and their position (job) within their herd. Whether it is foraging for food, social interaction or on look-out, there is seldom time to become bored. However, in their modern environment boredom can be commonplace when mental stimulation is lacking; this can lead to behavioural changes and vices such as crib biting (chewing the stable door or fence post), and weaving (stabled horses moving their heads from side to side). You will find some ideas to combat boredom in the chapters 'The Horse's Surroundings' and 'Gear and Equipment Explained', but right from the beginning examine the amount of time that can be devoted to your horse (you can use the time budget tool in the *Entwined* toolkit at oceaneasy.net).

## Human emotions and the horse

Anthropomorphism or the projection of human traits when describing horses is commonplace in the horse world. We all do it! Here is a snippet from a social media post from our yard, Ocean Easy Stables.

14.40 I was alerted to a problem on the yard by a whinny from Dantes, (head of herd cohesion). Don V (head of security) had found a breach in fence effectivity on the Garden Paddock quadrant. This was confirmed by the sighting of a large equine rump framed by the Ocean Easy Stables office window. Spritz (health and safety officer and neighbourhood watch coordinator) was quick to point out the potential hazard of the hay baler should the security officer venture further down the driveway. After acknowledging this potential danger warning Don V changed direction to inspect the laundry and was apprehended and taken to a secure paddock. Meanwhile Swish (entertainment officer) thought this was a brilliant stunt and well worth a flashy trot around the paddock despite the heat of the day.

There is of course no harm in talking about a horse's character in terms of recognised human characteristics or behaviours so long as we realise that this is only a human perception and the horse remains a horse!

As mentioned in the previous chapter, controlling human emotions (which equates to chemical and nervous energy, actions and consequences) around horses is very important. The truth is that a horse's brain is capable of cognitive processes (evaluating and learning) but **not** of reasoning as we know it (cognitive studies are continually being undertaken all over the world to improve our understanding of the horse's mind). A white shirt surely means no nose rubbing? That just does not compute in the horse's brain unless careful training has taken place with particular cues. They are not reasoning beings like humans and this fact cannot be stressed highly enough. They do not plan or hold a grudge; they act and react 'in the moment'. This is something that my coach instilled in me at the very beginning of our coach/student relationship, a fact of horse behaviour that I am so thankful she emphasized so strongly. A handler, rider or trainer needs to set their emotions aside and react appropriately! Stop, think then act.

## The horse's comfort needs

There is much spoken and written about animal welfare but what does horse welfare actually mean? Horses are sentient beings; they are capable of feelings and their comfort needs are simple but sometimes forgotten.

Within animal welfare studies and evaluations, the five freedoms are often quoted; they are the basis for veterinary practice and rescue centres, and should be the basis for every owner. All domesticated animals must be:

- **Free from hunger and thirst**
- **Free from pain, injury and disease**
- **Free from fear and distress**
- **Free from discomfort**
- **Free to display natural behaviour**

Freedom to display natural behaviour is necessary for good mental health and includes:

- **Social interaction (the need for companionship and tactile displays such as grooming)**
- **Feeding patterns (remembering that horses are trickle feeders, (grazing almost constantly rather that eating just once or twice a day)**
- **Play**
- **Uninterrupted sleep patterns**

If a horse is prevented from these natural behaviours it may begin to suffer from frustration-induced stress and of course boredom.

Let's take a look at social interaction, feeding patterns and the horse's 'down' time.

**Social interaction**

Horses are herd animals, company of the same species is incredibly important to them. If you plan on owning just one horse then arranging a paddock or stable buddy is imperative for their mental wellbeing as they will reply on their buddy to share the jobs such as 'look-out' duty within the herd. They will also look to their own kind for bouts of play.

Allowing horses the ability to touch each other to perform acts such as mutual grooming is also important. There is more on arranging your horse's space to allow for this in the chapter 'The Horses Surroundings'.

## Feeding patterns

As mentioned previously, horses are trickle feeders and should ideally have access to grazing or preserved forage, (such as hay, chaff or haylage) around the clock. This however, needs to be balanced with how much exercise or work the horse is doing and the type and quality of pasture and preserved forage. Additional feeding to meet the energy, protein, vitamin and mineral requirements of horses should be split into at least two feeds a day. Some competition yards may break this into three feeds if the work is intense and the amount of additional feeding high. There is more information on this topic in the chapter 'How the Horse's Body Works'.

## Sleep patterns

Horses need to sleep for around three to four hours in a 24-hour period, depending on physiological factors, such as their age, and environmental factors, such as weather and temperature conditions.

Horses will mostly sleep standing up (there is more information on how in the chapter 'How the Horse's Body Works') but will require short periods of sleep lying down either on their side or on their chest with their nose on the ground to experience REM sleep (the rapid eye movement phase of sleep, usually in short five-minute bursts). A horse may need to have periods of REM daily, or every few days, to prevent unwanted behaviours arising from sleep deprivation. Each horse is different.

The weather is probably the most influential factor for our horses and their sleep patterns. When living in a tropical region, thunderstorms and high rainfall can prevent them from REM for a while, even though shelter and a safe flooring are provided. Planning to minimise distractions that can cause a lack of sleep is highly recommended and making allowances is even more important. Let's face it, we can all feel a little grumpy and less tolerant after a sleepless night.

**A new take on horse welfare**

So, are the basic five freedoms enough? These have been revisited in recent animal welfare research by research scientist Professor David Mellor, BSc (Hons) PhD; he suggests that as horse owners we need to look at and plan for the following when examining how we care for the horse:

- **Equine nutrition** (forage and additional feeding)
- **The horse's environment**
- **Health**
- **Behaviour**
- **Mental stimulation**

Make a mental note to refer to this list as you read through the information in 'How the Horse's Body Works' and 'The Horse's Surroundings'.

## Motivation

Just like humans, horses need to be motivated to 'work'. Remember they are hard-wired to walk along with their heads down grazing for most of the time.

Some may be motivated by just enjoying human interaction while other horses may be motivated by food rewards. Each horse is different, so it is worth spending some time finding the right motivators for each horse so that both horse and owner can work as a team.

## Communication

One of the most common mistakes that you can make when communicating with your horse is assuming that they understand your language, whether it be verbal or physical.

Horses can't speak English, German, Spanish or any other tongue but they can identify with sounds (vibrations), and our body language.

Horses communicate amongst themselves with their body language as well as sounds and chemical excretions. The best way to understand a little of their behaviour is to watch and listen to their interaction with other horses. What will stand out when you examine them over time is that their communication is consistent, clear and rarely misunderstood by their herd.

Our goal should be clear and consistent communication with our horses. Therefore, human body language is incredibly important. Awareness of our own body cues and consistency goes a long way to effective communication with horses without the spoken word.

Personally, I talk quietly to our horses; I find it helps control my emotions. They pick up on my tone and I note from their body language that a low voice in certain situations helps to instil confidence in them: it has a calming effect.

When interacting with a horse, however calm they seem, remember for safety reasons to always be mindful of their natural instincts, i.e. fight and flight.

## Being aware of stressful situations

A horse's modern environment may produce many stressful situations, such as confinement when tying up or transporting (horses are claustrophobic by nature). This needs to be borne in mind and professional help sought if you are new to training a young or inexperienced horse. Refer back to the process of finding expert help to assist in managing the situation successfully, (horses are incredibly forgiving, but they never forget!).

In response to stress in their modern environment, the fight or flight reflex may be triggered (running backwards off the truck, or pulling back while tied up); they may also show signs of restlessness (fidgeting) or become completely immobile (freeze). Learning how to read what they are thinking or feeling is incredibly important.

There is a basic stress assessment tool in the *Entwined* toolkit at oceaneasy.net

## What is the horse thinking or feeling?

You can learn to understand what your horse is thinking or feeling by reading their body language. I was reminded by Georgia Bruce when collating this information that when interpreting your horse's body language, it is important to observe the whole horse: learn to look for clusters of body language signals, rather than over-generalising what one swish of the tail or flick of an ear might mean. There are a series of photographic cues from our super models, APH Swish, Cristogracia Dantes and Don Versprechen in the *Entwined* toolkit at oceaneasy.net

# HOW THE HUMAN
# BODY WORKS

## Mind/body control, language and systems

Body awareness is what this section is all about: identifying the systems that make us tick and identifying a level of control to make us more self-aware, both in and out of the saddle.

The human body is continually responding to stimuli and knowing how the body's sensory system works can improve our understanding of body awareness.

### The nervous system and senses

As mentioned previously myths are often mistakenly taken as commonplace wisdom. This is also true about human physiology; indeed, the notion that we have just five senses that feed into our central nervous system, brain and spinal cord is too simplistic to explain the many different physical reactions to a whole host of stimuli.

## Let's get technical!

There are 12 cranial nerves that emerge from the brain which receive and process information continually; there are also 31 pairs of spinal nerves outside of the brain which make up the peripheral nervous system, each of which can receive stimuli from the environment and the human body systems. This information is sent to the brain via a series of chemical and electrical signals.

To make this a little clearer, think of the prank where someone drops an ice cube down a friend's T-shirt. The recipient's brain will receive a chemical message from sensory nerves about the size, shape, weight and texture of the ice cube, but there is also a further set of sensory nerves associated with temperature that is giving signals to the brain all at the same time: in short, a complicated string of messages is sent in an instant to the command centre.

Understanding the previous scenario is relatively easy but understanding the human body's true abilities can more complicated.

The magic of spacial awareness is something that is often taken for granted. How can the proximity of all our body parts be mapped in relation to the environment? For example, how can a simple task such a touching the top of the left knee with the top of the right index finger with eyes closed be achieved? Did you just try this?

There are receptors within human muscles fibres called 'spindles' that tell the brain about the length of our muscles in relation to their stretched state; with this information from the sensory system, it is possible to subconsciously move the body around in our space appropriately.

There are useful tricks that the human body routinely performs, such as orientation: which way is up? The fluid in the inner ear helps to balance our head movements allowing us to focus on the environment without losing balance or experiencing that awful nauseous feeling, a big help when sitting to the trot!

**Biomechanics, the musculoskeletal system**

What does human biomechanics mean? Put simply it is the understanding and application of engineering mechanics in relation to the skeletal and musculature systems of the human body.

Combining knowledge derived from experts in the field such as sports physiotherapists and equine sports coaches can offer a greater understanding and improve posture and rider body position. These will influence effectiveness in the saddle, ultimately enhancing performance and enjoyment.

The correct body position in the saddle will obviously differ with the different disciplines and sports (e.g. the showjumper vs the barrel racer), the level of training of the horse, and saddle or pad used. Having body awareness in relation to biomechanics and the knowledge of correct posture and positioning will go a long way to enhancing time spent in the saddle and reducing the risk of sports injury which can extend mobility for many years.

**Body awareness and communication**

Awareness of body position on the ground is as important as in the saddle, not only to improve posture and injury prevention but also to control body language and reflexes around horses.

Did you know that a horse can learn to tell a handler or rider's mindset as soon as they approach the paddock gate just by learning to read human body language? As stated before, it is important to remember that horses are not born with the ability to 'read human' but with repetition they pick up our signals remarkably quickly. It is our responsibility to teach the horse signals and aids consistently for ease of understanding and cooperation. Remember the basics of how horses learn and be quick to praise and reward when the desired behaviour is offered.

If we are developing a new relationship with a horse, whatever the horse's age, we must take the time to understand what cues that horse responds to. An understanding of the language used from a previous handler or rider will go a long way to avoiding confusion and make for an easier transition into their new way of life.

Don't underestimate the importance of getting to know each other on the ground first before sitting in the saddle; each action from the handler will have a reaction from the horse! Often it is safer to understand their 'buttons' on the ground first before venturing into the saddle.

Body awareness in the saddle is paramount for a relaxed and rewarding experience.

Body position is part of body language and you can ask a horse to translate coordinated movements with your weight and pressure (aids)—for example, a desire to move forward, a command for halt, or indeed moving our horse's body in a myriad of different ways. However, it is also important to realise that we can believe we are asking for a certain action but unintentionally block the action from happening with our own poorly aligned position. We may also give inconsistent cues, which will most likely result in an incorrect response. Far too often the horse is reprimanded for the incorrect response when it is of course the rider's fault. Another important message from my coach that I will never forget is, 'Look to yourself first, fix that, then see if the horse is responding correctly.'

So, to reiterate, if the reaction was not what is expected, it is likely to be a miscommunication, a misunderstanding or inability to act; that means it's time to revisit body awareness and seek expert help.

Knowing how to influence the body by awareness of mind and muscle control is invaluable to us as handlers, riders and trainers. With the knowledge of how to stimulate specific muscle groups and physical training it is possible to achieve a near automatic and fluid sequence of actions to achieve correct body positioning in and out of the saddle, influencing both body language and effectiveness as a handler, rider or trainer.

**The core muscles**

The core muscles are referred to frequently in the fitness industry and horse-riding literature but what are they?

Exercise Physiologist **Sarah Tomlinson** explains:

> The core refers to a collection of muscles in the lower trunk area which contract together to form a corset of muscle around the abdomen. The deep core muscles include the pelvic floor, transversus abdominus and multifidus.
>
> The function of your core muscles is to provide support and mobility and it is from the core that all your body movements originate. If the core muscles are not working together effectively, other muscles in the body can overcompensate which may cause fatigue and injury.
>
> Identifying, triggering and developing the core muscles with regular targeted exercise will help your posture, strength, mobility and balance.

**Dominance, asymmetry and balance**

Discussing the sensory system and the core muscle structure of the body offers more of an insight into how we use our bodies. However, everyone is asymmetric by nature: there is a favoured side for thinking, writing, kicking a ball, and even seeing. Generally, a right-handed person will be left brain dominant. Conversely, the right brain of a left-handed person tends to be dominant.

Knowing what is involved can help us work on symmetry for better balance, position and coordination.

There is a dominance tool available in the *Entwined* toolkit at oceaneasy.net

**Cardiovascular and respiratory systems**

As with any activity in life a healthy cardiovascular system is important. Making sure that aerobic exercise is part of our exercise routines will help keep our bodies in good shape. Whether it be High Intensity Interval

Training (HIIT), exercising at maximum effort for short periods of time with a period of recovery (for example 30 seconds high intensity with 1 minute 30 seconds recovery); weight training or slow and steady exercise. Direction from a fitness professional for a recommended routine in line with age and fitness level is imperative.

**Effective breathing techniques**

As riders, the importance of correct breathing cannot be over emphasised. We communicate with our horses, not only with our bodies, but also through our breathing rate and breath placement: controlling both how we breathe and the rate at which we breathe will influence not only our horse's body but also our horse's mind.

Changing our breathing to rapid short breaths when we become anxious about a situation on the ground or in the saddle will often escalate the problem by signalling to our horse that their flight mode should be on standby and they should be ready to react!

Conversely, learning to breathe deeply, contracting and relaxing the diaphragm (expanding the rib cage on a breath in and slowly expelling the air fully), will instil confidence in a horse both on the ground and when we are in the saddle, encouraging the horse to relax and listen to our cues.

## Nutrition

This is an area that is easy to neglect, as we often consider our horse's nutritional requirements before our own. There is more information to come on the horse's digestive system and their nutritional requirements but here is an outline of our human body basic nutritional needs.

The human digestive system incorporates both physical (the breaking down of food parts) and chemical (the breaking down of food by digestive enzymes) systems.

The food we eat provides our bodies with energy and nutrients. We measure energy in kilojoules or kilocalories (calories for short) and we use around 1 calorie per minute when sitting down relaxing. So probably a relaxing trail ride is not all the exercise you need!

Foods are made up of:

**Carbohydrates** (molecules of carbon, hydrogen and oxygen atoms).

These are basically sugars (sucrose, fructose, glucose and galactose (monosaccharides) and starch (disaccharides and polysaccharides, glycogen and cellulose), which our bodies use to create energy, but which will, in excess, cause the body to lay down fat.

Carbohydrates are classified using the **Glycaemic Index (GI)**. This classification system also records the effect of each individual carbohydrate foodstuff on the body's blood glucose levels (blood sugar). Blood sugar peaks about 30 minutes after the foodstuff is eaten, returning to fasting level in about 90 to 180 minutes.

- **Low GI value—55 or less**
- **Medium GI value—56-69**
- **High GI value—70 or more**

High GI foods (simple carbohydrates) are foods that break down quickly in the body and cause a rapid rise in blood glucose levels (an energy burst) but, remember with the highs come the lows. After the burst of energy has subsided the body will be left feeling tired very quickly after the sugar spike. Be very careful of sugars hidden in processed foods and don't forget that most fruit contains a lot of sugar.

Our brains need 100 grams of glucose per day so eating some carbohydrate (which is also present in meat and vegetables) is important for brain power as well as physical activity.

Low GI foods are good for keeping blood glucose at a median level for long periods of time and giving sustained energy throughout the day.

Our bodies also need **fibre** for a healthy digestive system, which is available from the cell walls of the plants that we eat (cellulose).

**Proteins** (molecules of nitrogen, carbon, hydrogen and oxygen atoms)

Simple proteins (monomers) join to form polymers (chains of **amino acids**), which are required for cell growth and repair.

There are around 20 different amino acids available in food. Amino acids are classified as essential (must be supplied in the diet) and non-essential (which the body can make from absorbing proteins). **Essential amino acids:** Leucine, Isoleucine, Valine, Threonine, Methionine, Phenylalanine, Tryptophan and Lysine.

If you are eating a balanced diet with meat, fish, eggs, dairy, nuts and pulses your protein needs will be covered, but bear in mind that not all proteins are equally digested.

When protein is broken down by the body and used as fuel the nitrogen element is removed by the kidneys.

**Fats** (molecules of carbon, hydrogen and oxygen atoms)

Fats are categorised as saturated or unsaturated, depending on the numbers of fatty acids present. There are two essential fatty acids needed in our diet:

- **alpha linolenic acid (n-3)** (from sources such as canola oil, pumpkin seeds, walnuts)
- **linoleic acid (n-6)** (from sources such as sunflower oil, nuts and seeds)

Our bodies can make other fatty acids from these.

Triglycerides (3 x molecules of fatty acids and glycerol) are obtained by digesting the fat in your diet. They are needed to insulate your body and make cell membranes and are also released from the liver to meet short—term energy needs. When consumed in high levels the excess is stored as body fat.

Fat is also needed for the body to absorb the vitamins A. D, E & K.

As an energy comparison:

- **1 gram of carbohydrate (starch and sugar) provides 4 calories**
- **1 gram of protein will provide 4 calories**
- **1 gram of fat will provide 9 calories**

## Minerals and vitamins

Already small enough to enter the body through the intestine they do not need to be digested, though they may be converted to more readily absorbed forms; once ingested they are absorbed into the bloodstream. If eating a healthy balanced diet supplementation is seldom needed.

**Minerals** are needed by the body for many functions such as forming bones and teeth, and are important constituents of body fluids and of enzymes that break down food and body tissues.

Some minerals are needed in large amounts (e.g. calcium, phosphorus, magnesium, sodium, potassium and chloride) and others in much smaller quantities (e.g. iron, zinc, iodine, fluoride, selenium and copper).

**Vitamins** are required by the body in small amounts. As mentioned previously there are fat-soluble vitamins (A, D, E and K) and there are also water soluble vitamins (C, B1, B2, niacin, B6, B12 and folate). Water-soluble vitamins need to be consumed more frequently as they are eliminated from the body faster than fat-soluble vitamins (which are absorbed through the lining of the intestine and accumulate in the body).

**Water**

Correct hydration is vital, especially as around 70 per cent of our body's non—fat mass is water.

There is no medical research to say exactly how much to drink and this will depend on age, exercise, temperature etc. An easy way to tell if your body has reached full hydration is by taking note of urine colour—pale or clear is an indication of a fully hydrated body.

**A balanced diet** is essential for a healthy body and keeping the balance when you are time poor or under stress (such as trying to balance a home/work/horse lifestyle or at a competition venue) can be difficult.

The three main things to remember are:

**Avoid carbohydrates that have a high GI rating**—you may benefit from the immediate sugar rush but the energy spike won't last long. There is also the risk of long-term health problems such as diabetes. Reaching for that chocolate bar or cake may seem a good idea at the time but it will not sustain your energy for long.

**Beware of low-fat options**—low fat does not necessarily mean low calorie as the fat is often replaced by sugars.

Eat a variety of **protein-rich foods** and **complex carbohydrates** to give the best balance for your health.

**Safety**

Looking after your body in the horse world is also about not taking risks. There is more information about risk assessments and protecting our bodies later in the chapter 'The Horse's Surroundings' but here are a few key things to be aware of.

**Protecting the spine is essential.** We need to be mindful of how we use our backs in and around the yard as well as in the saddle. With bags of horse feed weighing 20+ kilos, heavy horse manure and aggregates to move around, using safe lifting procedures is a must.

Here's how to lift a heavy load:

- **Bring the object as close to you as possible**
- **Make sure you are facing the object (toes, knees and upper body)**
- **Place one foot alongside the object and bend your knees**
- **Keep you back upright as you lower and prepare to lift (don't bend at the waist)**
- **Engage your core and stomach muscles then tuck your tail bone under**
- **Lift the object and slowly straighten to an upright position**
- **Move your feet (don't twist your body) to change direction and re-position the object**
- **Keep the object close to you as you move it and prepare to set it down**
- **Bend your knees, position your feet as for the lift and keep your back straight as you set down the load**

Use the same procedure for lifting the handles on a laden wheelbarrow.

Use mechanical help where you can or ask for help to share the load.

**Body protectors** are designed to look after your spine if you should sustain a fall. Some styles have additional protection for shoulders.

**Wearing a helmet is a sensible decision.** Whether you are handling a horse on the ground or are in the saddle. Remember, horses' reactions are far quicker than our own and wearing a helmet may save a life.

**Wearing closed-in shoes** or boots can also save feet from broken bones and bruises. When a horse steps on toes they invariably will not notice—all they will feel is uneven ground!

**Protecting the body from over-exposure to the UV rays of the sun** is easily done by wearing long sleeves, or UV-inhibiting sun protection shirts and sleeves; these options look after the skin and the environment without using harmful chemicals such as sunscreen.

**Eye protection** is vital. Choose a shatter-resistant lens with UV blocking properties in a wrap-around frame for optimum protection.

**Protecting yourself from disease** is also important. When attending a sick or injured horse wear personal protective equipment (PPE) and be aware of biosecurity procedures in your area. Make sure hand-washing facilities are on the yard, and ensure that human and equine tetanus vaccinations are up-to-date.

Also check with the local vet that your horse is protected with vaccinations recommended for your area to prevent transmission of diseases.

# HOW THE HORSE'S BODY WORKS

**Nervous, endocrine, musculoskeletal, respiratory, circulatory, digestive systems and everything in between**

Understanding the horse's body is what this chapter is all about. Identifying the areas of the horse and having a basic understanding of a horse's body systems will help with monitoring and caring for a horse's wellbeing.

Understanding the terminology used for a horse's body parts or 'points' of the horse will unravel a whole new language which will help with communication, relaying and understanding important information while interacting with a vet, farrier or other equine health professionals as well as other horse enthusiasts.

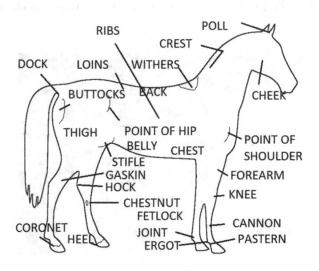

You can also refer to the *Entwined* toolkit at oceaneasy.net for diagrams on the points of the horse and their body systems.

## Let's get technical!

It should now be firmly engrained that a horse's reaction time is a fraction of ours! A horse may be alerted by a visual stimulus, smell, taste (taste and smell are very closely related), a sound or touch; their subsequent reactions are governed by their nervous system and their endocrine (hormonal) system.

It helps to bear in mind that a human presence and every action that the human may make around a horse will stimulate a reaction. The reaction may not be obvious, so it should become a habit to look for responses and changes in behaviour, building an awareness of the reactions that are caused. This will go a long way to understanding what makes an individual horse tick.

### The nervous system

Like the human body, a horse's body has a central nervous system (brain and spinal cord) and a peripheral nervous system; which consists of nerve bundles extending out from the central nervous system to the body and limbs.

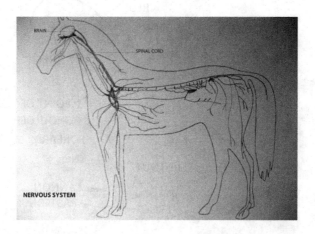

There are basically two types of nerves: those that bring messages into the central nervous system and those that carry messages out.

Nerves that carry messages out are either somatic or autonomic. Somatic nerves run directly to the cells in a horse's muscle to send signals to contract or 'activate' that muscle, while autonomic nerves make connections through synapses in cell clusters called ganglia. The autonomic nerve connections are made to smooth muscle, such as those in the horse's blood vessels and glands.

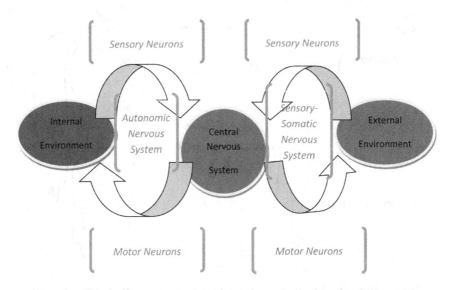

Somatic and autonomic nerves are very fast acting, so when a message is received, such as a stimulus that the horse is in imminent danger, the response is rapid.

The sensory nerves that send chemical messages to the central nervous system are found everywhere in the horse's body. They give feedback on their own body in the form of muscle movements, the position of relative body parts (spatial awareness), skin sensations, as well as sending messages about their environment (such as temperature).

## The endocrine or hormonal system

This system is not as fast acting. The endocrine glands produce chemical messages which are released into the bloodstream to target certain areas and organs of the horse.

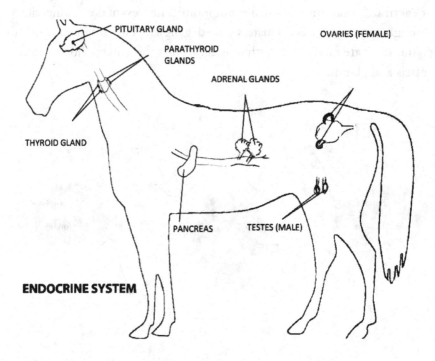

Although hormonal responses are slower to form, they are longer lasting.

Did you know that horses excrete chemical messages in their dung? This is why some horses want to stop and sniff other horses' dung.

## Biomechanics, the musculoskeletal system

What does equine biomechanics mean? Just like the human body, it is the understanding and application of engineering mechanics in relation to the skeletal and musculature systems of the equine body.

Why is this topic so important?

A good place to start is by selecting a horse with the correct biomechanics for the job as this will make for a happier horse/human partnership. Asking a heavier horse type such as a warmblood to perform on the racetrack, for example, would not be an ideal scenario: it simply does not have the right biomechanics for the job.

Understanding how horses are put together (type and conformation) is very important: seek expert help and guidance when selecting a horse. Start with a veterinary check where a qualified vet will be able to give an opinion on the suitability of a given horse's biomechanics to match a chosen sport or pleasure pursuit. A reputable breeder will also be able to give advice as breeding programmes aim to produce the ultimate biomechanics (as well as other factors such as temperament) for a given sport or discipline.

A good breeding programme limits conformation issues, (how the musculoskeletal composition of the horse is put together) that may lead to physical restrictions: it is designed to produce horses with optimum performance potential.

Knowing how a horse moves in relation to their gait and footfalls is also important, as it will help in spotting changes in their movement, highlighting possible unevenness or soundness issues. It will also add to an understanding of equine biomechanics when in the saddle.

Horses' feet should be viewed as part of the muscular/skeletal system. Paying a great deal of attention to a horse's feet will assist with their balance and movement. Whether their feet require just trimming regularly (approximately every six weeks) or shoeing (at a similar time frame), horses' feet need expert care and regular maintenance.

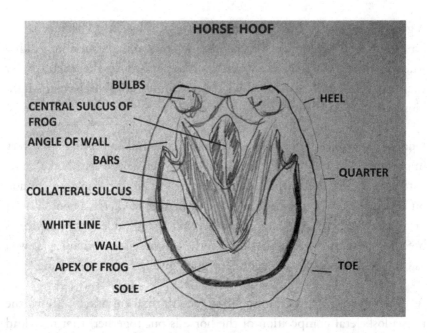

HORSE HOOF

BULBS
CENTRAL SULCUS OF FROG
ANGLE OF WALL
BARS
COLLATERAL SULCUS
WHITE LINE
WALL
APEX OF FROG
SOLE

HEEL
QUARTER
TOE

Imagine the effect it would have on a human body if the person was to walk in a pair of shoes with uneven heel heights? Their musculoskeletal system would begin to compensate by using muscles incorrectly, placing undue force on their skeletal structure and it is no different for a horse!

It is incredibly important to seek out an experienced, qualified farrier—'no foot, no horse'!

**Sleep mechanism**

A horse will sleep around three to four hours a day and will do most of their sleeping standing up. So how can they nod off without falling over? To keep themselves upright horses have an amazing 'stay apparatus' in their forelegs (a function of their tendons and ligaments), and a 'check apparatus' in their hind legs which allows their weight to be distributed on their forelegs and one hind leg, resting the hoof of the other hind leg on the toe. There is a 'hook' structure on the inside bottom of the femur at the stifle joint; a certain rotation of the horse's hip will lock the patella triggering the medial patella which results in the 'stay function' of the hind legs.

## Dominance, asymmetry and balance

Just like humans, horses are not built symmetrically, which leads to the dominance of one side with certain parts of their body. The biomechanics of a 'good or bad side' are a little complicated for the relative newcomer to the horse world; that is where a qualified horse health worker, trainer or coach, well informed on equine biomechanics, will help you to understand a horse's asymmetry and teach you how you can help the horse develop better balance and a more even way of using themselves. This ultimately will, as with the human body, assist with reducing injuries and extending mobility as they age.

Be mindful that when you ask a horse to work, either during ground work or in the saddle, it may be a little harder for them to give the desired movement that was asked for on one side rather than the other. Take advantage of expert advice with training and schooling to help the horse work in a balanced manner, getting them to use their muscles equally on both sides.

Also remember that a rider in the saddle will alter the horse's balance. Staying still, balanced and effective in the saddle is a quest every rider should be working towards: whether it is the occasional trail ride or on a show jumping track, balance for both horse and rider is the key to a happy, harmonious riding combination.

## Communication: visual, auditory and tactile

The importance of human body language and the importance of clear and consistent cues (aids) have already been mentioned. Horses interpret information from humans as well as assessing their surroundings through many different sensory mechanisms.

Vision is one of the horse's sensory mechanisms which differs from our own. The placement of the horse's eyes on either side of their head gives them excellent peripheral vision but conversely, they do not have very good binocular vision or depth perception (judgement of distances of objects and depths of obstacles, such as changes in the ground cover). Something that seems simple to us such as a dry to wet area of sand can be hard for a horse to interpret, and if their judgement in the past has proved them wrong then they may display extra caution at a similar object or obstacle the next time. So, there may be a very good reason for hesitation at that puddle! Horses galloping through water have either learnt that it is safe from following their herd or by trusting their handler, rider or trainer.

Horses have a visual system that is a little like an in-built bifocal lens. Robert Miller, DVM, a US veterinarian, concludes that this allows horses to change focus from near to far in a fraction of the time it would take a human eye to adapt. He also detailed that the top part of the horse's eye is used for near vision, hence dipping their neck and head to inspect close objects. Conversely, the bottom part of the eye is used for distance vision, which supports the reasoning for the raised head as part of the flight response posture.

Be careful of a horse's blind spot, directly in front of their head and behind their tail, making sure that your presence is known by approaching the horse from the side well outside of their blind spot.

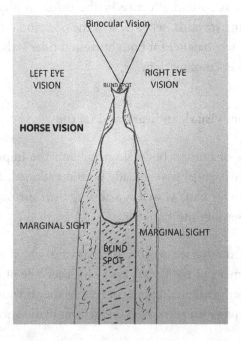

Horses' eyes are a very sensitive area and should be protected against excessive dust or excessive UV light.

Unless compromised, your horse's hearing acuity is incredibly sensitive with an ability to detect a large range of frequencies with a far greater capability than a person. Their ears are designed like mini satellite dishes to pick up the tiniest sound. The signals that we may miss—a twig that cracks underfoot some distance away, or the tall grass that is displaced by another animal—emit a high frequency sound, which a horse's ear is attuned to. Watch for the ear turn, known as the **Preyer Reflex**. This can alert us to the fact that the horse has heard a sound and is ready to react, time for us to make a distraction to diffuse the situation!

Your horse's sensory receptor nerves in their skin stretch right up into the surface, although skin thickness and therefore the density of nerve fibres vary over different areas of the body. This sensitivity also differs from horse to horse and from breed to breed (the Thoroughbred generally having a thinner skin type to, say, a Clydesdale). Take time to know and examine an individual horse's sensitivity.

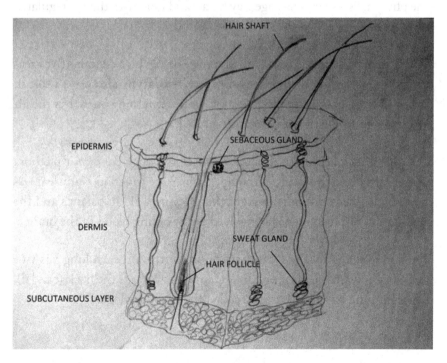

## Respiratory system

When a horse breathes in, the air passes into the nostrils, up through the nasal passages and over two bony rolls in the cavity called conchi. The air continues through the pharynx, larynx and into the trachea passing through the guttural pouches before finally arriving at the lungs.

The horse's nostrils can increase and decrease in size (depending on how much air/oxygen is needed) by expanding and contracting the cartilage around the nostril area.

Their airways play an important role in the prevention of disease: horses' nostrils are coated with tiny hairs that remove particles of dust and debris, while their nasal passages are coated with a lining of mucous which helps to humidify the air on breathing in. The bony rolls of the conchi within their nasal cavity increase the surface area allowing cool air to circulate and increase in temperature before proceeding on through their respiratory system.

The pharynx is a shared passage way for air and food with the use regulated by a flap of skin, called the soft palate, and the larynx.

The air then passes over the larynx (the voice box) which contains five areas of cartilage, allowing the horse to vocalise. The larynx also plays a role in controlling the passage of food/air and, while remaining open, lets the air pass through to the trachea (breathing tube).

The guttural pouches are unique to the horse; they contain a plethora of nerves and blood vessels, although their exact function is unclear. As they are air-filled sacks it is thought that they may aid in balance and the equalisation of pressure, or be involved with cooling blood to the brain.

The horse's lungs are the final destination for the air: each lung has two lobes, one towards the front (cranial), and one towards the back (caudal). The right lung has a further lobe called the accessory lobe.

The movement of a horse's lungs is helped by their diaphragm muscle. As the diaphragm flattens, the air is drawn in, moving the rib cage out. Conversely, as the diaphragm moves up the ribs move in, and they expel the air into the atmosphere.

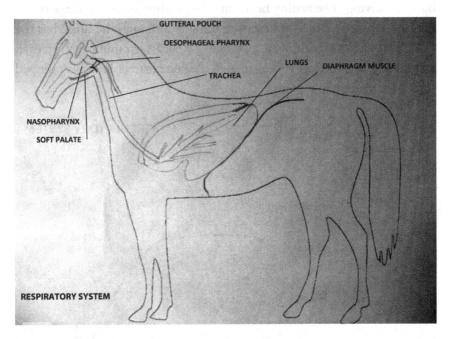

GUTTERAL POUCH
OESOPHAGEAL PHARYNX
LUNGS
DIAPHRAGM MUSCLE
TRACHEA
NASOPHARYNX
SOFT PALATE
RESPIRATORY SYSTEM

There are two major considerations for a horse's respiratory system; air quality and head position.

Air quality entering a horse's body is paramount. Limiting the dust from bedding, working areas (such as sand arenas) and paddocks is imperative for healthy lungs. Making sure there is adequate ventilation in enclosed areas such as a stable or horse float/truck is also important.

It is also essential to note that when a horse is grazing its head should be held in a 'natural' position. The head and neck must be in a position to 'drain' the nasal passages. For this reason, horses should not be restricted from maintaining their natural grazing position (head and neck lowered) for more than four hours at any given time—working, competing or transporting—as this can compromise their respiratory system.

## Circulatory system

The circulatory system of a horse, which includes the heart, spleen and vascular system, must cope with an enormous demand for oxygen when a horse is moving. The resting heart rate, (depending on size and age of the horse) is between 20 to 40 beats per minute, although the horse has the capacity to increase their heart rate up to 250 beats per minute. With each contraction of the heart it is estimated that one litre of blood is pumped through the vascular system.

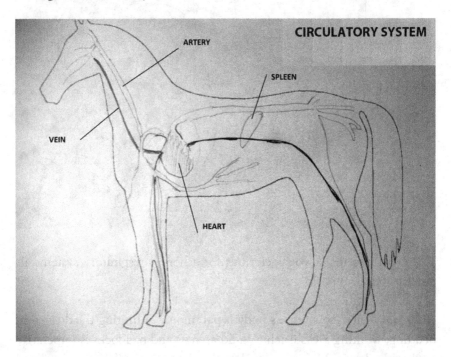

Located in the chest cavity, known as the mediastinum, the heart sits in the lower two thirds of the thorax extending from the second or third rib to the sixth. The horse's heart is similar in structure to a human's but is approximately 1 per cent of their body weight; for an average 500 kilo horse that would mean a 5 kilo heart. However, this percentage does vary slightly with the breed of horse.

Many studies have been conducted on the size of a horse's heart in relation to their athletic ability; it is generally considered that the larger the heart the better the athlete, so not surprisingly, the Thoroughbred horse generally has a larger heart relative to their weight when compared to other breeds such as the heavy horse types.

A horse's vascular system consists of arteries that carry oxygenated blood and nutrients away from the heart, through to the capillaries situated within the body tissues (muscles, skin etc.).

Veins travel from the body tissues back to the heart.

A horse's spleen is the key to how their circulatory system can react so quickly: it not only removes damaged or diseased white blood cells but also stores red blood cells when they are not required.

When an average sized horse is in a relaxed state and therefore the spleen is relaxed, it can hold approximately 30 litres of blood (the horse has around 50 litres of blood within the body). When the horse is in a state of excitement or stress the spleen contracts to allow approximately 25 litres of blood back into the bloodstream, reactivating the stored red blood cells so they can deliver more oxygen to the organs and muscles quickly to power the fight or flight mechanism!

**Digestive system**

The horse is a non-ruminant herbivore, as is a diverse range of animals from mice to elephants. Despite many myths, horses are not like cows (which are ruminant herbivores) and have very different digestive systems and nutrient requirements.

A horse uses both enzymatic digestion and fermentation to process nutrients within their bodies.

Let's look at the parts of the digestive system:

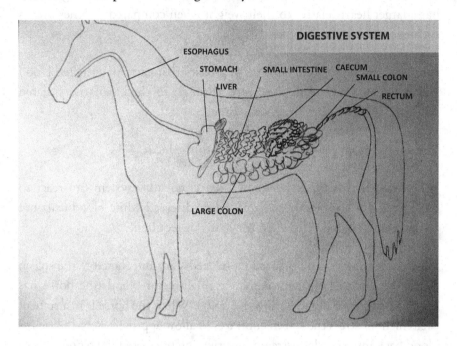

## The mouth

The lips are used to forage for food and the tongue used to direct the food through to the teeth. Horses' teeth are an important part of their digestive system; the incisor teeth tear the pasture or forage whilst the pre-molar and molar teeth grind the feedstuff.

The horse's head and neck position when feeding will have a direct effect on the wear pattern of the teeth (as does the type of feed that they are eating). Choose your horse's feed container and placement carefully (more of this later). Regular dental check-ups (annual or more frequently, depending on age) are required to maintain horse health and comfort.

It is very important to note that a horse needs to chew to produce saliva; unlike humans, they do not salivate at the sight or smell of their food!

The saliva produced both lubricates and 'buffers' the food; the buffers are a combination of electrolytes that helps to control the acid balance of their food through their digestive system.

With 16 to 20 hours of chewing the volume of saliva produced can be as much as 40 litres. It is not hard to see that access to a clean, fresh water supply is a must.

After the horse has chewed the feed sufficiently, mixed it with saliva and swallowed, it passes through to the food tube (oesophagus). As you will recall from the respiratory system there is a series of valves (flaps of skin) that prevent the food from passing into the horse's larynx (voice box) and trachea (breathing tube).

The oesophagus is approximately 1.2 to 1.5 metres in length (obviously depending on the size of the horse—think of the different length of their necks). The wall of the oesophagus has a series of smooth muscle fibres which contract at intervals in a motion known as peristalsis; these contractions move the food bolus (the small, rounded mass of chewed food) along the tube and down into the stomach. Any obstruction here can cause 'choke', which is another reason why fresh water should be constantly available to your horse.

**The foregut**

The stomach is the first part of the horse's foregut; it is about the size of a football, (again depending on the size of the horse), is relatively inelastic and can hold around 8 to 15 litres in volume, though the shape of the stomach means that it is usually no more than two thirds full at any one time.

When feeding a horse, consideration needs to be given to the quantity in each feed, making sure not to overfill the stomach, otherwise the feed will pass into the small intestine before it has been processed by the stomach acids. This can cause discomfort for the horse as it inhibits the correct digestive process, but it is also a waste of money for those purchasing the food as the nutrients in the feed will neither be absorbed properly nor used efficiently. As a rule, a feeding rate of half a kilo per 100 kilos of horse is standard. A horse's ration may need to be given in several feeds: hence 'feed little and often'.

If feeding additional complete feeds (feeds that contain all of the horse's energy, protein, vitamin and mineral requirements) or concentrates/balancers (to meet vitamin/mineral requirements) it is important that you read the feed label for guidance. Horses should have constant access to forage (pasture or preserved forage such as hay) unless their condition is too good (overweight), in which case their intake must be managed carefully for optimum health; veterinary recommendations should be followed if this is the case.

A horse's stomach is divided into two compartments separated by a band called the margo plicatus. The food bolus first passes into the top squamous section, a non-glandular area which is given protection from the strong stomach acid by the buffering effects of the saliva and the physical barrier of the fibrous portion of the horse's feed. This is one of the reasons why access to forage is important for horse's gut health.

The bottom of the stomach, the gastric section, is glandular: the glands secrete a mucous which protects the stomach wall against the hydrochloric acid produced. The pH of the stomach reaches around 1.5 to 2 and this acidic environment breaks down the feedstuff into simple components before being passed through to the small intestine; there is very little absorption that takes place in the stomach—it can be thought of as more of a processing plant.

The small intestine is small in diameter but not in length! Depending on the size of the horse it can range from 21 metres to 25 metres and makes up around 75 per cent of the total gastrointestinal tract. It can hold around 60 litres of food which pass along its length by peristalsis at around 30 centimetres a minute.

The small intestine is where enzymatic digestion takes place. The enzymes secreted from the pancreas break down the food matter to allow it to be absorbed into the bloodstream.

The food matter is buffered to a pH level of around 7 to 7.5 to protect the delicate inner wall lining. The liver provides bile to protect the sensitive villi and microvilli (small protuberances that line the intestine which increase the surface area for maximum absorption).

Did you know that horses do not have a gall bladder? A gall bladder stores and concentrates the bile produced by the liver, but as the horse is designed to eat constantly the bile is in constant demand and therefore no storage is needed.

The small intestine has three areas: the duodenum, the jejunum and the ileum. Each of the areas has a specific function through the digestive process.

It is important to remember that the horse's small intestine is designed to have feed constantly passing through; interruptions along the large length of the small intestine should be avoided by feeding little and often and allowing access to forage (unless they are under veterinary supervision).

**The hindgut**

The large intestine takes its name from its circumference rather than its length. In total the horse's large intestine is approximately 7 metres long (depending on the size of the horse) and makes up a huge 60 per cent of the gastrointestinal tract volume carrying around 125 litres.

Progressing from the ileum of the small intestine the foodstuff passes through to the caecum of the hindgut with a valve preventing backflow to the foregut. The caecum is sometimes referred to as the fermentation vat: there are no digestive enzymes produced in the hindgut but there is a plethora of mucous secreting glands, bacteria, protozoa and fungi that break down the fibre content of the feed (microbial digestion) releasing volatile fatty acids to produce energy and heat.

It is not unusual to see a horse's forage intake increase in cold weather or reduce slightly in warm weather due to the by-product of heat produced in the hindgut. In cold conditions, it is therefore imperative that adequate roughage is available for the horse to maintain core body temperature. There is more information on retaining the horse's body temperature later.

From the caecum, the fibrous foodstuff passes through to the horse's large colon (again named because of the circumference rather than length); fermentation and absorption takes place in the right and left ventral and dorsal bends of the 3 to 3.5 metre structure. It is here that colic due to compaction is most likely to occur/arise if hydration or trickle feeding is compromised.

The horse's large colon leads into the small colon where the faecal balls are formed before moving through to the rectum and being expelled through the anus. Water is re-absorbed from the small colon which helps to maintain adequate hydration.

It is incredible to think that much of the water that is drunk—which helps to produce the 35 to 40 litres of saliva daily and lubricates the foodstuff—allows it to travel approximately 30 metres before being absorbed by the horse's body. This highlights again the necessity for free access to clean, fresh water for both gut health and adequate hydration.

## Measuring weight and condition scoring the horse

There are three generally well accepted methods for estimating your horse's bodyweight:

- **Weight tapes—you place a specially marked tape around your horse's girth and it gives you an estimated weight**

- **Weight and condition score**—using your horse's height and body condition score and a published weight table, you can look up your horse's estimated weight
- **Girth and length measurements**—measuring the horse's girth and length from point of the shoulder to point of the buttock and then enter them into the equation:
- **kg of bodyweight = [girth (cm)$^2$ x length (cm)] ÷ 11,880**

The last method is thought to be more accurate.

When assessing the condition of a horse these areas are taken into consideration:

- **Behind the shoulder**
- **The ribs**
- **Along the neck**
- **Along the withers**
- **Along the crease over the loin**
- **The tail head**

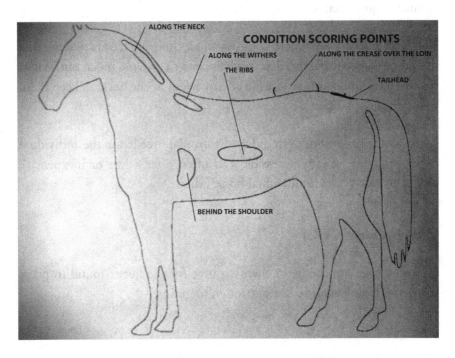

There are several different systems you can use to identify a horse's condition. A local veterinarian often has charts available. There are also charts available from feed manufacturers and on the internet.

## Nutrition

The horse's energy comes from a combination of carbohydrates (sugars and starches) and fats/oils.

As mentioned previously, the horse evolved to graze. However, our modern lifestyle means there is often a lack of adequate pasture or sufficient quality available to supply enough energy for the level of work that may be asked of the horse.

Therefore, additional feeding by using preserved forage, such as hay, chaff and haylage or fibre replacements such as soybean hulls and sugar beet pulp can be formulated in a ration together with complete feeds or concentrates/balances to sustain energy levels, protein, mineral and vitamin requirements.

The most important thing to consider when choosing feed is that the diet should be correctly balanced: it can be as bad to give too much nutrient as too little! It should also reflect the energy needs of the horse to keep them in optimum condition.

Equine nutritionists understand and formulate feeds for the individual horse—they are readily accessible and often offer a free or inexpensive service to help plan an individual horse's diet.

### Carbohydrates (CHO)

Carbohydrates are the main energy source for the horse; found in plant structures from pasture grasses through to grains.

Fibre is the structural component of the plant or grain. Referred to as cellulose, it consists of multiple glucose molecules strung together in a rod like formation to give the plant, seed or grain structure. There is more on the energy source of fibre later.

Non-structural component carbohydrates (NSC) include sugars and starches.

These include the water-soluble carbohydrates (WSC: fructans, glucose, fructose and sucrose). On horse feed packaging a percentage figure relating to WSC is sometimes given; this will indicate the percentage of sugar carbohydrates within the feed but it will not give details with regard to starch or fructans that cannot be broken down by enzymatic digestion in the foregut and may cause issues when digested in the hindgut.

Starch is a CHO that is not soluble in water at standard room temperature; grains in particular contain a high percentage of starch.

**Dietary fibre**

Fibre is important for gut health in the horse: it keeps the digestion process moving along the gastrointestinal tract. On reaching the hindgut, digestion via a fermentation process releases volatile fatty acids, a form of sustained energy for the horse. Each plant, grain or seed has a fibrous fraction, but pasture, preserved forage, soybean hulls and sugar beet pulp are where most fibre is found. Soybean hulls are regarded as 'super fibres' as they can be digested more readily than hay, chaff or beet pulp in the hindgut. It is important to select good quality forage: make sure that the hay or chaff is not too stalky as it may contain high amounts of lignin, (an organic polymer that gives structure to the plant as it grows) which a horse cannot digest. Look out for moulds and dust which will affect not only the horse's digestive system but also their delicate respiratory system.

Feeds that incorporate a high fibre content replicate a more natural diet for the horse.

**Fats/oils**

A horse's natural diet includes small quantities of fats from forage. However, the horse tolerates this energy source well. Fats, (generally fed as oils) offer a slow release energy, although attention to the correct balance of the fatty acids (omega three, six and nine) is needed. This has already been taken into consideration in quality complete feeds. If in doubt seek the advice of a qualified equine nutritionist.

**Protein**

Proteins are the building blocks of the horse's body. They are required for many different functions: structural (muscle, skin, hair), enzymes, hormones, and compounds for the immune system and transportation systems throughout the horse's body.

Proteins are made up of strings of amino acids and each part of the horse's body requires its own code of protein through different stages of maturity. There has been a great deal of research in the horse world to determine the right 'quality' proteins for the horse: not all proteins are the same and not all feedstuffs contain the right proteins in the right quantities. Seek advice from an equine nutritionist to make sure that you are feeding quality proteins.

**Vitamins and minerals**

The horse needs a balance of vitamins and minerals for optimum health. Once ingested, vitamins and minerals are absorbed directly into the blood system. It is very important to find the correct balance for an individual horse as too much of one vitamin can counteract another. The best place to start planning a horse's diet is with an equine nutritionist.

**Water supply**

The need for constant access to clean, fresh water has been highlighted several times in the section on digestion. It is an important nutrient for the horse and care should be taken to make sure that their water supply is not contaminated; a good rule is that if you would not drink the water then it is probably not suitable for your horse! You will find more information on this topic later.

## The health check

Making routine checks are a key to avoiding trouble but it is necessary to know what is 'normal' for each individual horse so that there is a baseline for comparison. Construct the horse's baseline measurements by making a thorough check of the horse from head to hoof, noting locations of lumps, bumps, scars, markings and the like. It helps to record these for future reference and guidance for all the horse's carers.

Be aware of the horse's vital signs (a guide is available in the *Entwined* toolkit at oceaneasy.net): there is a 'normal' range but it is a good idea to see where each individual horse fits in the normal range. If in doubt about the health of a horse call the vet immediately!

### The healthy horse

Previously it was highlighted that there is a number of animal welfare guidelines. Keeping a horse free from illness and disease is a responsibility not to be taken lightly.

Vaccines are available for specific equine disease prevention. Protection against tetanus and strangles. These should be administered to a horse annually to prevent painful and in some cases fatal diseases. Some countries require horses to have an annual flu vaccine and depending on where you live other vaccines or government health regulations may be appropriate. Discuss this issue with a local vet and review any government requirements accordingly.

Parasites are always present in the gut of a horse and a horse's worm burden needs to be identified and managed. Taking a sample of the horse's dung to a vet for analysis, (where they can conduct a faecal egg count) is a quick and effective way of measuring the worm burden and identifying the types of parasite affecting the gut. The vet will be able to give advice on the best treatment regime with a regular worming programme, as some areas may have drug-resistant worms. Parasite management is covered in more detail in the next chapter 'The Horse's Surroundings'.

Horses are often bothered by flies, some of which may bite, carry diseases or be the cause of open sores. In some areas, ticks are also a problem. Prevention is always better than cure and you will find more about fly and tick protection later. Vet advice should be sought for the treatment of open wounds or itchy lumps.

An annual equine physical is recommended which may include temperature, heart and respiratory checks as well as assessing gut sounds. A thorough check may also include an eye examination, sheath cleaning, hoof evaluations, dental checks and advice on nutrition following body condition scoring.

# THE HORSE'S SURROUNDINGS

This chapter looks at some of the most common external influences on the horse in relation to their modern environment. There has already been some information on the horse's evolutionary environment; here is a short reminder of the facts. It is important to realise that in today's world a horse is expected to adapt to our lifestyle and a balance needs to be found between meeting a horse's comfort and welfare needs and our convenience.

## The evolutionary environment

When a horse is displaying natural grazing behaviour it will cover large areas of pasture land, sometimes up to 26 kilometres a day and grazing would take up much of the day (16 to 20 hours); rarely do we provide the space and quality of grazing to match this natural state. The horse is not a solitary animal; it is a herd animal and displays natural behaviours such as mutual grooming and play.

## Let's look at the modern paddock environment

When choosing a paddock environment for your horse there are many factors to take into consideration.

## Companionship

As horses are herd animals, companionship of the same species is incredibly important to them. In fact, in some European countries, legislation has now come into place to ensure that a horse is kept at least within eyesight of another.

When information on the horse's mind was previously examined, we touched on their behaviour as prey animals including the fact that they can internalise stress or pain so as not to draw attention from predators. It is important to note that just because a horse is not vocalising (calling out to other horses) it does not necessarily mean that it is secure and comfortable in isolation from other horses! Companionship leads to a freedom from fear and distress, one of the five freedoms discussed in the chapter 'How the Horse's Mind Works'.

Companionship also counteracts boredom. Horses have a job to do within the herd which keeps them thinking in their social environment.

Horses kept together will form their own hierarchy and within the dynamics of the herd scuffles can sometimes happen. If injury is a major concern (such as with performance/competition horses) you will often see them fenced in separate paddocks adjacent to one another. The ability for your horse to see and touch a neighbouring horse is important to fulfill social needs, but this arrangement with the safest fencing possible can also help to manage injury risk.

## Paddock size

Depending on where you live, space can often be difficult or expensive to acquire, which in turn can lead to too many horses and not enough paddock (overstocking). Ideally the stocking rate should be in the region of one horse per five acres of good quality pasture, but of course smaller paddock sizes are commonly seen. Paddocks need careful management regarding resting periods, soil health, seeding, watering and drainage, along with manure and pest management.

With less than adequate pasture, additional feeding in the form of preserved forage such as hay, chaff and haylage or a fibre replacer in the form of soybean hulls or sugar beet pulp will be necessary; depending on your horse's energy requirements; complete feeds may also need to be given incorporating the energy sources, vitamins and minerals required. If the energy (including the protein requirements are met), a concentrate or balancer may be given to supply the vitamins and minerals lacking in the pasture. An equine nutritionist can advise on the correct balanced diet for a given horse.

## Pasture

Identifying and understanding the nutritional properties of the grasses and legumes within a horse's pasture is very important. Different grasses and legumes have different nutritional benefits and drawbacks for horse health.

Some cool climate grasses, such as rye, contain fructans. A fructan is a non-structural carbohydrate made up of molecule chains of fructose that horses cannot breakdown by enzymatic digestion in the small intestine (you can refer back to the equine digestive system covered previously). Fructans pass through to the horse's hindgut to be broken down by microorganisms, this produces lactic acid and in large quantities can upset the pH balance in the hindgut leading to an environment where the microbiome cannot thrive. This can cause discomfort for the horse which may in turn lead to health conditions such as colic or laminitis. If your horse is susceptible to laminitis (a painful inflammation within the hoof which disrupts the blood flow to the sensitive and insensitive laminae) careful management of grazing times in relation to plant fructan production (which is linked to temperature, plant syntheses and growth) must be understood and considered.

Some tropical grasses contain oxalates, acid molecules that bind with the calcium in the plant; if present in pasture they will prevent a horse from absorbing calcium which can lead to a calcium deficiency. This is obviously cause for concern for bone and cartilage health and can have dire consequences. For more information and assistance with identifying the components of your pasture contact a local agronomist.

Horses are picky eaters and will often graze on their favourite areas leaving bare patches and longer tufts (called roughs) of their 'not-so-favoured' pasture. Mowing paddocks to an optimum grazing height of approximately 12 to 20 centimetres (topping the paddock) helps to avoid this. Aim to use a third of the paddock area at any one time to allow areas of grazing rest and growth periods; avoid overgrazing when planning the paddock environment.

**Weed and toxic plant management**

As well as identifying pasture you will also need to identify weeds and plants that are toxic to the horse. The Department of Animal Science at Cornell University has an online guide to poisonous plants for livestock and an easy reference using both the scientific name and the common name of the plant.

To help with weed identification refer to your local or national environmental government agency. In countries such as the UK and Australia there are government online resources available to assist with identification.

Weeds can be invasive when areas of pasture have been nibbled down to the roots, but they can be removed manually or by spraying. If you are using a spray then seek advice from your local agronomist or agricultural supplier on its suitability for your pasture and read the manufacturer's guidelines. Ensure you are aware of how long you will need to keep your horse off the pasture once sprayed and check that you will not cause any adverse effects on the environment, especially regarding drainage into waterways. It is also worth noting that a chemical spray will change the chemical structure of the plant or weed: what may have been unpalatable to your horse prior to spraying may now be more appealing, so make sure they are not ingesting sprayed weeds. You will also need to protect yourself if using chemicals; this is discussed further in the final chapter 'Gear and Equipment Explained'.

## Soil management

A healthy paddock needs a healthy base. A professional soil test will identify which nutrients are present and which are lacking. Soil testing can also give important information regarding the suitability of growing certain grasses and legumes.

When looking at types of soil, a clay soil will be high in nutrients but gives cause for concern with drainage. Sandy soils are generally lower in nutrient value and can dry out relatively quickly. It is possible to test the pH balance of your soil with a gardener's soil test kit. A neutral pH level is recorded as a 7, with acidity increasing as the number lowers; above 7 the soil is alkaline. Both acidic and alkaline soils can be deficient in minerals which may lead to poor growth of pasture. A local agronomist will be able to assist you with improving the soil and selecting the right pasture management plan.

## Irrigation and drainage

Incorporating drains to direct water flow is necessary in areas that receive high rainfall. The ability of the soil to drain is also very important to avoid puddle formation and slippery areas within the paddock. Clay soils are notoriously bad for drainage—adding gypsum (calcium sulphate) will help to aerate the soil and reduce impaction, as does managing where your horse is standing or loafing when not grazing. Sandy soils are generally better draining, but critical nutrients can be lost with high rainfall, so adding organic matter rather than just liquid fertiliser to sandy soils is necessary to improve soil fertility. A local agronomist will be able to advise on a soil management plan.

If you live in an area with limited rainfall for all or part of the year you will need to instigate a water management system and may consider installing an irrigation system for paddocks and exercise areas. Irrigation will obviously help with pasture growth and can also cut down the amount of dust that a horse is exposed to. Dust can be a real threat to a horse's respiratory system as dealt with in the chapter 'How the Horse's Body Works'.

## Gates and loafing/sleeping areas

Attention needs to be paid to high-traffic areas, such as gateways, and areas around shelters where a horse will stand (loaf) and sleep. Bare soil will become compacted in these areas and the pasture coverage will be non-existent. It is worth 'sacrificing' these areas and separating them from grazing (with a gating system to allow freedom of movement when grazing is available) so that pasture can be preserved and managed.

Adding aggregates to gate areas will improve the footing, especially in areas receiving high rainfall. There are also recycled plastic cells available that can be buried into the soil in gateways and filled with aggregate; these have proven to help with soil stabilisation. Make sure if you are using these cells that they are well covered and will not cause injury or rubbing if a horse chooses to lie down over the area. Ensure that you offer a suitable bedding material in the shelter area so that is their first choice.

## Manure management

If your paddock is relatively small, removal of dung should be done at least daily. Removing manure from the pasture has several benefits:

- **Increases the areas of grazing (horses will not eat around the areas where their manure is spread and 'toilet' areas can develop quickly in paddocks)**
- **Assists in controlling your paddock's worm population (and in turn will have a positive effect on your horse's worm burden)**
- **Also helps to control flies in the warmer seasons**

Of course, the downside of manure removal is the removal of nutrients from your paddock, so if you are planning on collecting and utilising dung as organic matter in soil management, talk to an agronomist about preparing, fertilising and resting paddocks using manure as part of your paddock management plan.

If you can rest paddocks or areas of your paddock you can improve the nutrients in the soil by harrowing, which involves using machinery to drag through the paddock and manure piles. This will disguise 'toilet' areas as well as benefitting pasture.

**Fencing**

Horses evolved with the freedom to roam so however careful we are as horse owners we cannot override the fact that horses and fencing don't mix!

There is a wide variety of fencing options available; above all the fencing needs to keep your horse securely within the area fenced with minimal risk of injury from the fence itself.

Wooden fencing needs to be of adequate height for your size of horse, taking into consideration the bottom rail height to prevent limbs being caught underneath when lying down or rolling. Be mindful that horses do like to chew wood (they will naturally graze on the bark of some trees), and a fence post or rail also acts as a great scratching post. Usually treated wood is not so palatable. Giving adequate fibre in a horse's diet will help reduce the urge for horses to chew a wooden fence.

Plastic fencing has become popular for aesthetics and ease of maintenance. Make sure that this type of fencing is adequately secured and will resist the weight of your horse pushing or rubbing. Electric fencing is also a popular option. The electric wires can be coupled with either wooden panels (which can avoid the horses rubbing) or with plastic fencing, it can also be used between wooden or metal fence posts using plastic or rubber insulators. Electric braid is also an affective option rather than wire but will degrade over time, especially in sunnier climates.

Fencing using star pickets is popular as temporary fencing to segment paddocks. A plastic cap should always be securely fastened over the top of the picket to avoid injury to the horse.

Although any type of fencing can cause injury, especially if a horse takes flight and runs into the fencing at high speed, barbed wire should always be avoided. Such fencing can cause horrific injuries if a horse should become tangled in it.

Before taking on the expense of fencing an area seek advice from equine fencing companies and contractors. They will be able to assess your requirements and offer the safest and most effective solution for the horse's individual needs.

**Shelter**

A horse requires some form of shelter from the elements. The worst conditions for a horse to manage combine wind and rain, but in warmer climates shelter from the sun's rays is also needed.

Take into consideration the aspect of the shelter.

- **Will it offer protection from the sun all day?**
- **Is the opening to the shelter away from the usual direction of the wind and rain?**

Enough shelter needs to be offered for all the horses housed in the paddock. Take into consideration behaviour within the herd (who buddies with whom) and plan shelters accordingly.

Shelter can take the form of natural barriers such as a bank of trees, though this can be hazardous when winds are high with the risk of falling debris. Trees also house bird and bat life and as you will read later there can be some health concerns relating to this.

Man-made shelters should be of a solid construction which limits the risk of horse entanglement, cuts and abrasions. The shelter needs to be of adequate size so that a horse is not at risk of being cast (getting stuck), if they choose to lie down. It also needs to be of adequate height to limit head injuries should a horse rear in play or in defence from their companions.

If the shelter is constructed from tin it should be lined with a suitable material such as stable grade rubber or marine ply that will be thick enough to withstand a kick from a horse (the force from a horse kick can punch through tin causing injury).

Pay attention to the shelter flooring: while this will depend on the climate and conditions, the area needs to offer a dry section to stand without it being too abrasive—ideally not too hard—to alleviate strain on tendons and joints.

Horses can sleep standing up, but they do need to lie down to experience a period of REM sleep. If they choose to do this in the shelter the flooring needs to offer a level of comfort that does not cause sores or abrasions to the horse's skin (this usually happens around the hock area). Pay attention to gaps between the shelter walls and the flooring and make sure that they are not large enough for a horse's hoof/leg to become trapped.

The final form of shelter is of course rugging. This will protect the horse from the elements and you will find more information on this in the final chapter 'Gear and Equipment Explained'.

As mentioned in the discussion on pasture, if you can offer shelter for your horse to stand and loaf away from grazing it will preserve pasture and avoid tracks and areas of bare soil.

**Water supply**

Water is vital for the horse and a clean, fresh water supply should be available at all times within the paddock/shelter area. A horse will normally drink between 30 to 50 litres of water a day (depending on the size of the horse, their diet and the weather/temperature).

Placing the water under shelter can help protect against contamination from bird and bat droppings and leaf litter.

Make sure you regularly clean the bucket/trough to ensure that contaminants are removed, and algae formation is reduced.

Also be careful to monitor the temperature of the water. Horses do not like to drink if the water is too hot or too cold. A good rule is: if you would not drink the water then why should your horse?

Consider the type, colour, size and positioning of your water trough:

- **Will it hold enough water?**
- **Does the colour affect the temperature of the water (black will absorb the light/heat)?**
- **Will the trough be too heavy or difficult to drain and clean when full?**
- **Can the trough be placed to avoid contamination and also drain for cleaning without flooding the pasture/shelter?**

## Let's look at the modern stable environment

The amount of paddock time available to a horse can be determined by the pasture available and their job: for instance, on a competition yard, if a horse is in 'full' work, it may be considered more convenient to stable the horse and manage their available paddock time around their work schedule. However, each horse is different, and energy levels and characters should be considered when determining the amount of paddock time required for a healthy body and state of mind. Pasture management will also be a key influence on stabling.

### Planning the stable

When choosing or building a stable for your horse there are many factors to take into consideration:

- **The location in relation to other stabled horses, paddocks, exercise areas, and if the stable is based on your property, is it in the most convenient place to monitor the horse?**

- The direction in which the stable is facing: when will it receive the sun and is it protected from the elements?
- Your horse's view: does your horse have an entertaining outlook, are they able to see/interact with their companions?

You can avoid stable boredom and undue stress on your horse by taking these things into consideration at the onset.

## Materials

Like a shelter, the stable needs to be constructed from materials that will be able to contain a horse without increasing the risk of injury. Stables are usually of wood, brick or tin construction.

The stable needs to be lined with a suitable material, such as wood, marine ply or stable grade rubber, thick enough to avoid cuts and abrasions and withstand a kick!

## Size

The size of the stable needs to allow for adequate movement and should be able to accommodate your horse lying down with ample room to prevent your horse from becoming cast. Pay attention to the height and width of the stable door; make sure that your horse can see comfortably over the door and that the width allows your horse to enter and leave easily.

If the stable is to be made available to your horse from the paddock, make sure that the doors are retained securely with minimal risk of your horse becoming entangled. The bolts and fastenings should be easy to use and offer a level of security with the ability to release them quickly. It is amazing how many horses quickly learn to open stable door bolts! A kick bolt at the bottom of a stable door can be a great feature for added security.

## Flooring and bedding

The flooring of your stable needs careful consideration. Concrete is a good base, but a further covering must be used. It is possible to cover a concrete base with stable grade rubber matting. Both concrete and rubber are easy to disinfect and hose down.

There are a variety of bedding materials available ranging from straw to sawdust and modern products such as hemp and paper. When considering a bedding material, you need to take into consideration:

- **Is your horse likely to ingest it?**
- **Is the material absorbent?**
- **Is the material readily available?**
- **Is the material affordable?**
- **Is the material the best option to do the required job?**
- **Will the material create dust that may affect your horse's respiratory system?**
- **Is the material free of pathogens and other harmful substances?**
- **How easy is it to muck out, clean and replace?**

## Water supply

As discussed in the paddock environment, you will need to be able to offer your horse an adequate, clean and fresh water supply for their time of confinement in their stable. Water buckets are an obvious choice but must be placed to be accessible without being knocked over. Some horses like to play in their water and an automatic water feeder in each stable is a good option to avoid this and keep the water supply fresh. It needs to be placed at the correct height and situated so it is both accessible but limits your horse from either harming themselves or breaking the unit. It must be cleaned and maintained daily to avoid them failing. If the unit uses a power supply (not gravity fed) it must be uninterrupted (something to consider if you live in an area with regular power cuts).

The ability to monitor water consumption must also be taken into consideration. It is easy to assess how much water a horse is drinking when buckets/troughs are being used. Most automatic re-filling troughs and automatic waterers generally do not have the facility to monitor daily water consumption. Water is a vital component in the horse's digestive system: if a horse is not drinking adequate amounts their health will be impacted.

**Turn-out**

The amount of time a horse spends in their stable environment is dependent on many factors: occupation, state of health, weather conditions, grazing availability, etc.

Unless there is a contra-indication to health requirements (e.g. box rest for an injured horse) exercise and/or turn-out time in a paddock is essential. Always take into consideration the horse's social needs and offer a companion either in the same paddock, if they are compatible, or in an adjacent paddock to avoid injury.

## Boredom and cognitive enhancement

Boredom in the paddock or stable environment can lead to vices such as crib biting and weaving. To limit the development of vices, make sure that you supply the following:

- **Adequate turn-out time (if in a stable environment)**
- **Hand grazing (if limited turn-out for health reasons)**
- **Adequate forage (pasture or preserved forage)**
- **Companionship**
- **Exercise**
- **Cognitive enhancement such as paddock and stable toys**

## Feeding

Attention should be paid to **when** and **where** you feed the horse. A horse's behaviour may change around feed time: they could become more animated and aggressive towards paddock mates. Horses are, however, creatures of habit that respond well to a routine.

To avoid scuffles and to ensure that your horse receives their full ration (and only their ration!) feed the horse away from any companions.

Feeding away from the paddock in a dedicated area, (a sacrifice yard) can limit tracks in the paddock and wear and tear on areas around gates where horses tend to stand and wait for feed.

Try to feed at the same time of day and feed little and often, spreading the horse's ration over two or possibly three feeds. Feeding little and often is also a good boredom prevention tool.

Remember to match the horse's feed ration to their workload and energy needs to aim for optimum condition: if unsure contact an equine nutritionist for further advice.


## Exercise areas

Depending on where you are keeping your horse you need to consider the exercise environments that are available to you.

- **Do you have facilities such as an arena, riding/jumping paddock or round yard available to you and if so, are they regularly maintained and in good condition?**
- **Could you ride outside of the property in a relatively safe environment such as green lanes and trails with limited interaction with other road users?**
- **Consider other hazards such as barking/chasing dogs, other horses running fence lines, or unfamiliar noises such as plant and machinery**
- **Riding with a companion is a good practice. If a horse is new to you or the environment they are kept/ridden in, you may need to find some help with habitualising from an experienced trainer (or at least a confident riding buddy with an experienced horse)**

## Tie-up areas and wash bays

When taking a horse from the security of their paddock or stable environment to an area for grooming or tacking up, pay attention to the environment of the tie-up areas and wash bays.

If you are tying a horse up, can they still see their companions or most of the action that is happening around them? Remember a horse's visual system is highly sensitive to movement; placing the tie-up areas and wash bays facing the action can help to reduce stress (both human and horse). Addressing what may seem to be a small detail may reduce unnecessary tension and restlessness in the horse, making time spent on the ground with your horse far more pleasurable.

Assess tie-up areas and wash bays for possible hazards such as slippery flooring. Remove rakes and forks propped up in close proximity that can be knocked over or trodden on should the horse make a sudden move.

## Transportation

Horses are claustrophobic by nature; it is against every natural instinct of the horse to walk into a small area with no obvious sign of escape or to be enclosed in an often low-lit and noisy environment, so consider your horse's transportation with care. Take a ride in the horse's standing quarters before they are asked to enter (where safe to do so on private property) so you are aware of the experience the horse will have.

Make sure you receive professional help when asking your horse to travel for the first time. Taking your time and making the first experience a pleasant one pays dividends in the future.

Make sure you know the road rules and insurance regulations regarding your choice of horse transport. You will also need to be familiar with weight and licensing restrictions for horse trucks/lorries.

You will need to know the weight of the fully loaded float or trailer, which can be measured at a public weighbridge.

## Climate and weather changes

Be prepared for changes in the weather as well as adverse conditions that can affect your horse. Assess the climate where you live and the changes that are likely to impact on your horse's environment.

During the summer months pay attention to the UV index. Sunburn can occur on any pink (non-pigmented) skin region of the horse. A horse's skin is usually protected by the hair coat, but the areas at the end of the nose and around the eyes are susceptible to sunburn. With continued exposure there is a potential for the skin cancer, squamous cell carcinoma which can be very aggressive and difficult to successfully remove.

If the area you live in is likely to be affected by fire, flooding or strong winds make an emergency action plan ahead of time so that you are prepared for a safe outcome. Government agencies often offer assistance with emergency planning procedures.

Be mindful that horses are very sensitive to changes in climate and weather conditions. Monitor their health and vital signs (use the vital signs guide in the *Entwined* toolkit at oceaneasy.net) and take note of any alteration in their behaviour. Look out for large temperature changes, an increase in humidity, night frosts and wind chill factors and make sure they can maintain their core body temperature with adequate shelter/rugging and forage intake. Check their feed and water intake daily.

## Wildlife and pests

Within the paddock environment your horse may be exposed to local wildlife and pests.

Make sure you are aware of what wildlife and pests (such as wild dogs or bats) could visit your horse's paddock and any hazards that may arise. Does the wildlife pose a threat for your horse's health? Some animals carry diseases that may be transferred to your horse; insects may also be a nuisance, and some can carry disease.

Check with your local government agencies for possible threats to your horse's wellbeing, and your vet for advice on protection measures. Several physical protection measures are covered in the final chapter 'Gear and Equipment Explained'.

## Equine hospitals/veterinary surgeries

Sooner or later your horse will need a visit from the vet. In some cases, the vet will attend your horse in their paddock/stable environment but be prepared to visit the equine surgery or hospital. In this situation, your horse will be in expert hands but make sure that your horse has been vaccinated against any form of disease likely in your area, as there may be limitations on admission to a veterinary practice in an emergency situation for an unvaccinated horse. Contact your vet for details of protection for horses and handlers.

## Training and competition/show venues

If you are planning to travel for training, shows or events be prepared for your horse to be more 'aware' of the environment. Horses are incredibly sensitive creatures and each horse has very individual reactions to a new environment. If you are visiting an unfamiliar area to take part at a show or event, try to expose your horse to the venue prior to the event: it will help your horse to be relaxed in their new surroundings on the event/show day.

## Risk assessments

The key to considering your horse's environment is identifying and managing risk; risk for the horse and handler takes into account both mental and physical welfare.

It is a good idea to regularly walk through your paddock, stable and exercise areas and identify potential hazards for you and your horse.

You can take this further and look at your daily routine with your horse, breaking this down into individual tasks and identifying any potential hazards.

Once the hazards have been identified the next step is to calculate the risk and then, if necessary, act to reduce or eliminate that risk.

Here is an example:

- **Location: Tie-up area**
- **Hazard: Fork and wheelbarrow close to area**
- **Risk: Medium risk of horse becoming caught up in the hazard**
- **Consequence: Injury to horse**
- **Action: Remove and store fork and wheelbarrow next to feed container**
- **Risk: Minimised**

If you are planning a trip with your horse, spend some time on a risk assessment both for your travel itinerary and for the environment at your end destination. Reducing risks will make for a much happier experience for you and your horse.

You can find help with risk assessment by accessing the *Entwined* toolkit at oceaneasy.net

# GEAR AND EQUIPMENT
# EXPLAINED

This chapter looks at some of the most common saddlery and equipment needs of your horse, gear and protective equipment for the handler, rider or trainer and maintenance tools for the equine environment. Today, there are many technologies and inventions to help with horse management, most designed to be more effective while others will be convenient. It is important to consider the cost of that convenience both in monetary terms and in finding a balance between your lifestyle and meeting your horse's comfort and welfare needs.

## Let's take a look at the tack room

Whether you have a dedicated tack room or a corner of the garage, shed or bedroom there are certain items that you cannot do without.

### Halter and lead rope

If you are handling your horse you will need a halter, which can be made of leather, webbing, rope or synthetic materials; you must consider both the safety and comfort for your horse when making your choice.

For safety, consider being able to use the halter to control your horse effectively without causing harm or the halter breaking; for comfort, make sure that the halter fits correctly, and the material does not rub or cause your horse discomfort. Do not forget to keep your halter clean, and check for wear and tear regularly; if the stitching is loose or buckles broken, repair or replace them as soon as possible to avoid injury.

Lead ropes are also made from different fabrics such as cotton or synthetic materials; they are often braided or plaited for strength and ease of handling. Make sure that you choose the correct length for your horse (if your horse should stand on its hind legs will you still be able to hold the rope at a safe distance)? You may want to consider various lead ropes for different purposes, such as having a shorter rope at your tacking-up area and wash bay where you don't need long ropes dangling.

Choose a lead rope that is comfortable for you to hold and does not become slippery when wet!

**Saddle**

If you are riding your horse, you will need to consider what type of saddle or saddle pad you and your horse need. Different disciplines and sports have different types and styles of saddle.

The most important thing to consider is the fit of the saddle on your horse. Can you imagine walking around all day with tight-fitting shoes or walking in gum boots that are two sizes too big for you? Ouch!

The saddle must fit your horse correctly, sitting in the area behind their shoulder and in front of their last rib. The saddle must fit correctly over your horse's withers, along the back and under the cantle area (back of the saddle). The saddle will also need to be a good fit for you, the rider. A qualified saddle fitter can help you select the best saddle for you and your horse to ensure a correct and comfortable fit.

You will need to select a saddle pad (saddlecloth, numnah or saddle blanket) to place under your saddle; your saddle pad needs to be the correct size for your horse and saddle, should not interfere with the fit of your saddle and should exert 'no pressure' either at the wither or behind the saddle. The saddle pad, as well as adding to your horse's comfort, will act as protection for your saddle from horse sweat and loose hairs. Saddle pads are shaped for dressage, jumping and general-purpose saddles, as well as for western saddles.

## Bridle

You will also need to consider the type of bridle that your horse needs. Again, there are many different styles. The choice should **not** be made on looks alone—consider how the bridle works, and if a noseband is used, understand how it works (where it places pressure on your horse). Your bridle must fit correctly, not only to be effective but also to ensure that it does not cause your horse any discomfort. Ask a saddle fitter for advice or speak with your coach or instructor for help.

## Bit

Bits work by placing pressure on the structures of your horse's mouth; depending on the type of bit and the fitting, your bit may place pressure on the bars and/or roof of the mouth and/or the tongue area.

Each bit is different, and each horse's mouth is different. Seek advice from your saddlery expert, instructor or coach as to the most suitable bit for your horse (for their comfort and your safety); take advice on the sizing and fitting of the bit.

## Tack cleaning

To keep your tack in good condition you will need to clean it regularly (ideally after each ride).

Synthetic materials should be wiped down with a damp cloth and left to dry in a safe area, out of the sun, before storing.

Leather saddles and tack need a little more care: first, wipe off mud, sweat and hairs with a soft cloth, then apply a preparation such as saddle soap, grease and oil which in combination keep the leather soft and supple. Follow your saddle and tack manufacturers' guidelines as to which products to use—read the product care label carefully before use.

## Training aids

There are many items that fall under this heading from lunge lines to spurs.

With any training aid consider the following:

- **What result do you want to achieve with the training aid?**
- **Will the training aid do the job required?**
- **Are there alternatives?**
- **Do you know how to fit the aid correctly?**
- **Do you know how to use the aid effectively and safely, without causing harm to your horse?**

Again, ask your coach or instructor or help and advice.

## Boots, bandages and wraps

Boots and bandages are mainly used for leg protection. Trauma to horses' limbs can be caused by them knocking themselves as they move (usually at high speed or when making lateral movements), or by external factors such as knocking a rail when jumping or knocking a limb whilst lying down in the stable.

There is much debate as to how much support certain types of boots, wraps or bandages offer to the musculoskeletal system of the horse. Studies have also shown that it is possible to 'overheat' your horse's tendons with bandages and wraps on their legs for **long** periods of time during exercise.

When choosing whether to use a boot, wrap or bandage, consider the following:

- **Sizing to fit your horse's limbs**
- **Coverage of joints and tendons**
- **Support for joints and tendons**
- **Weight (as light as possible but still able to do the job)**
- **The amount of heat they will create/disperse**
- **Ease of cleaning and maintenance**
- **Ease of fitting**

Make sure that you understand the design of the boot and then fit it correctly. Boots can be lined or unlined and can be designed to fit the cannon bone, place over the fetlock or cover the pastern. Bandages should cover the length of the cannon bone stopping at the ergot (refer to 'How the Horse's Body Works' or the *Entwined* toolkit at oceaneasy.net for the points of the horse).

Fit the leg protection with the correct amount of tension: too loose and it will not offer support and may trap sand and dirt underneath, which can cause rubbing and sore areas on your horse's skin. Too tight and it may inhibit movement and blood circulation to the tendons.

## Grooming equipment

The basic grooming kit should include the following:

- **Hoof pick (for removing dirt and stones from the feet)**
- **Plastic curry comb (useful to remove mud)**
- **Water brush (to remove stains and lay the top of the tail and mane flat)**
- **Dandy brush (harder bristle—NOT to be used on the sensitive areas such as the head)**
- **Body brush (softer bristle for use all over the body and head)**
- **Metal curry comb (for cleaning the body brush ONLY and should never be used on the horse)**
- **Hairbrush (for the mane and tail)**

- **Mane and tail comb (used for combing through and pulling the mane. They are also useful when plaiting the mane and tail)**
- **Sponges (one for the eyes, one for the nostrils and one for the dock area)**
- **Stable rubber (soft lint cloth or similar for a final polish)**
- **Sweat scraper (to remove sweat after exercise and water after hosing down)**

With innovations in design, new materials and manufacturing techniques your grooming kit may look a little jazzier than the traditional collection of brushes, but the same principles apply. Make sure that you consider the sensitivity of your horse (refer to the chapter 'How the Horse's Body Works') and match the brushes and the pressure you use accordingly.

Ensure your grooming kit is cleaned and disinfected regularly. If you have more than one horse be careful of cross-contamination: you may want to consider separate brushes for each of your horses.

## Rugs

Rugs offer a form of shelter or protection for your horse. They are used to control your horse's core temperature, protect their coat as well as offering relief from the elements.

Rug types vary from thick winter rugs to keep out the extreme cold, rain sheets to keep your horse dry, to lightweight mesh rugs to keep your horse cool while providing insect protection. Quite often, (depending on the part of the world that you and your horse live in) you will need several rugs to choose from as the weather conditions and temperature change.

Fitting is important for your horse's comfort and to prevent the rug from becoming damaged; if they are too big or too small, or sit too far back on the horse they can cause rubbing, especially around the chest buckle and shoulder area. Loose leg straps and belly surcingles can be a hazard and may catch legs when the horse rolls, lies down or kicks out at a fly, often resulting in a torn rug and a repair bill or worse still, an injury!

You also need to be aware of your horse's temperature. The horse's thermoneutral zone (TNZ)—the range of temperatures that does not require the horse to expend energy to stay cool or warm, ranges between 0 to 25 degrees and depends on the climate they are used to. If the environment is cold make sure your horse has adequate forage to raise their core temperature (you can check your horse's temperature by placing your hand on the skin behind the point where the saddle would sit, the point of their kidneys), although research has shown that temperature checks from human judgement are not always reliable. If your horse is too cold to the touch and is eating more forage to help raise their core temperature, consider another layer or change the rug to one that will offer more insulation (this is often more comfortable for your horse rather than multiple layers) but try not to 'over-rug'. Horses are extremely efficient (given a good diet) at growing coats that are effective against the cold. However, this can cause difficulties if you are working your horse regularly. If the coat growth affects their temperature when working, you may need to consider clipping the coat and rugging accordingly. Balance their comfort against your convenience, putting your horse first.

If your horse becomes too warm, they may start to sweat behind the ears, neck and body and show signs of laboured breathing and lethargy. If your climate has cold nights and warm days make sure you remove the night-time rugs before the daytime temperature becomes too warm.

Your horse's rugs need to be maintained regularly; clean them by brushing off dirt and mud on the outside with a dandy brush and remove hairs from the inside with a softer body brush.

If they become caked with mud you may need to hose them down but check with the rug manufacturer on the best care routine for that rug. Some rugs are machine washable (a dedicated horse washing machine is preferable!) but be careful using detergents as some rugs, (such as rain sheets) come with protective coatings and you may need to avoid detergents in their care plan altogether.

Make your rug repairs in a timely manner; the saying 'a stitch in time saves nine' is very apt here! As you change rugs with the seasons make sure you repair, clean and dry rugs thoroughly before storing.

## Fly/insect protection

Flies can be an annoyance to your horse, but (as mentioned in the chapter 'The Horse's Surroundings'), they can also carry diseases. To protect your horse from fly bites you can use:

- **Rugs**
- **Fly masks**
- **Leg wraps**
- **Sprays**

Rugs are available with hood attachments, but make sure that they fit securely to avoid the hood slipping and rubbing your horse's eyes; some rug styles cover the belly area to offer more overall body protection.

Fly masks are available in different styles and materials. Ensure your horse can see out of the mask and that the material does not rub on their skin or protrude into the eye area. Fly masks can be made of a UV-inhibiting material that offers protection against the sun's rays for sensitive eye and nose areas.

Leg wraps can offer protection from biting insects. Make sure that they do not stop your horse's movement or rub the skin on their legs.

There are many sprays available to deter flies. Some use natural products, others use chemical compounds. Be aware of the active ingredients in the product that you choose and ensure that they do not irritate you or your horse; if you are competing with your horse, make sure you are aware of banned substances that can be present in some sprays.

## Let's look at the feed room

You may have a dedicated feed room, or like your tack room, it may be a shared area designated to storing your horse's preserved forage (hay, chaff etc.), fibre replacers (soybean hulls or sugar beet pulp), complete or concentrate feeds along with any supplements your horse may need.

Make sure the area that you choose is clean and dry. This will help to keep your horse's feed from becoming contaminated with fungal spores and mould.

To keep pests such as rodents and bugs away from your horse's feed either use a fully sealed room (such as a shipping container) or sealed feed bins.

Clean your feed storage area regularly, and disinfect and fully dry storage bins on a regular basis.

It is a good idea to include information of your horse's feed management in this area; using a white board is ideal as this can be amended when necessary. The information should include:

- **Details of feed (preserved forage, fibre replacers, complete or concentrate feeds, balancers and supplements)**
- **Quantities of feed components in each ration**
- **Timing of feeds (how many and when)**
- **Location of feeding (paddock, stable)**
- **Details of feed buckets to be used (placed on the ground, hung over stable door etc.)**

Your information board can also be used to show details on paddock management, including dates of worming and paddock harrowing. You can also record paddock treatments such as weed spraying and soil/grazing fertilising.

## Let's look at the horse's stable or shelter

A guide to selecting your floor covering was given in the chapter 'The Horse's Surroundings' but consider where you will store your horse's bedding material.

If you are using bedding such as hemp, shavings or straw you will need to have a dry, covered area for storage.

For clearing and cleaning the stable/shelter area you will need:

- **A wheelbarrow**
- **Brush**
- **Rake**
- **Fork**
- **Shovel**
- **Hose with water supply or buckets to wash down the stable**
- **A pressure cleaner can also be a useful tool**

Make sure you also have a designated area for spoilt bedding and manure and think about their disposal. Will you be using this to?

- **Mulch**
- **Compost**
- **Arranging for a contractor to dispose of the unwanted bedding and dung on a regular basis**

### Preserved forage, feed and water supply

When your horse is housed in the stable it will need feed buckets, a place for forage and a water supply.

Hay can be available to your horse in a fixed hay rack or manger, by using a hay net or, in preference, a hay-slow feeder. Make sure the rack or manger is fitted at the correct height for ease of use and to avoid injury (i.e. catching a limb); also consider the height of the fixing to avoid your horse rubbing and injuring itself or catching and ripping rugs. Think about entanglement with hay nets/bags: you may want to consider feeding hay at ground level in a suitable container such as a hay-slow feeder to allow the horse to feed with their head and neck in a natural position and so avoid the forage becoming mixed with bedding material.

Feeding at ground level is the normal head and neck position for the horse. If you are changing the height at which the food is delivered be mindful that this will change the action of their teeth grinding mechanism. This is one of the reasons that a regular dental visit is necessary.

You can either choose to provide water in buckets or by using an automatic watering system. Make sure either mechanism is cleaned regularly and if possible, with automatic systems, include a way of measuring your horse's water intake. Also make sure that if an automatic system requires a power supply that a back-up system is readily available in the event of power failure.

### Stable toys

To give mental stimulation you might like to consider placing a hanging stable toy. This can help to avoid boredom, especially if your horse is stabled for long periods of time. Hanging balls and devices that contain licks are popular but read the contents of the licks carefully as they may contain high levels of sugar which may alter your horse's health and behaviour.

## Let's look at the horse's paddock

For paddock management, you will need:

- **A lawnmower or slasher**
- **A harrow (if not removing manure)**
- **A wheelbarrow**
- **Fork**
- **Rake**

- Shovel
- Spray unit (if you choose to use this method for weed control)
- Hoses or water supply to clean troughs, buckets and automatic waterers
- Gate locks for security
- Emergency plan and contact information

Keeping your horse safe in a paddock environment is very important. Apart from details covered in the chapter 'The Horse's Surroundings', you may need to consider security measures with locked gates; do ensure that spare keys or lock combinations are given to several carers with emergency contact information clearly displayed on your emergency plan. You can place the emergency plan on the outside fencing of the paddock, out of the way of your horse (and their paddock buddies) but in view of other paddock users and the emergency services.

If you are feeding your horse in the paddock environment (preferably in a sacrifice yard), think about the feed bucket. Horses tip their feed bins for several reasons—eagerness or even vision? Be mindful that a horse prefers to see ahead when grazing/eating to watch for any danger. So, if you select a feed bucket that obscures their view, they may tip the bucket and eat from the ground to feel more 'secure'.

Pawing the ground is a natural behaviour to access tasty roots. The introduction of the feed bucket may trigger this behaviour so they may accidentally knock over the bucket. Placing the bucket in an old tyre can help to keep the bucket upright if your horse shows this behaviour.

If continual knocking over the feed bucket is a problem and placing it in an old tyre does not solve the problem, tie the bucket to a fence or shelter so that the feed can be accessed safely but be careful of entanglement.

As part of your worming management plan, you will either be resting and harrowing your paddocks or clearing your horse's paddock regularly. Make sure you have a dedicated area for manure composting/disposal, ideally a little way away from your horse's paddock to limit flies in warm weather. Also consider where the run-off goes in wet weather.

## Let's look at the horse's exercise area

The surface of your exercise area will dictate the care and maintenance required.

If it is a grassed area, it will require regular mowing and weed management; depending on the soil base it may require dressing with sand to help with the footing and drainage.

Sand arenas will require raking regularly to ensure an even footing. Irrigation may be required to manage dust and provide a surface that minimises concussion on your horse's legs.

To maintain the area, you will need:

- **A mower/slasher (for a grassed area)**
- **Rake (for a sand area)**
- **Watering system**

## Mounting blocks

Although you may be able to reach and step up into the saddle comfortably, there is a great deal of evidence that mounting from the ground places undue strain and pressure on a horse's spine. Using a mounting block limits this pressure and increases comfort for your horse.

## Horse shoes and hoof boots

The quality of your horse's feet, body conformation, exercise, as well as the climate, paddock and exercise surfaces will determine whether their feet would benefit from being shod or whether the use of hoof boots should be considered.

Many horses do well barefoot—your horse's welfare is foremost and you should seek the advice of an experienced and qualified farrier and/or vet to determine the best hoof care for your horse.

## Let's look at the horse on the move

Think about how you will transport your horse for:

- **Evacuation if needed in an emergency**
- **Regular veterinary/dental or farrier visits**
- **Training and competition**
- **Fun outings**

You will need to choose your transport with care and consider the following:

- **The structural integrity of the float, truck or lorry**
- **What is the ride like (will your horse be bounced around)?**
- **What is the noise level like?**
- **What is the ventilation like?**
- **Will your horse's muscles become stiff from draughts?**
- **Is the horse protected from bugs/debris entering the windows or vents?**
- **Does the flooring offer protection from concussive forces?**

You will also need to consider your horse's protective equipment when transporting:

- **Lower limb protection—float/travel boots**
- **Hock protection—hock boots**
- **Knee protection—knee boots**
- **Body protection—rugging (removing rugs before off-loading)**
- **Head protection—poll caps (to protect the top of the head area between the ears) and fly masks**

When transporting your horse make sure that you carry an **equine first aid kit** and that it is easily accessible should there be an accident (it may be a good idea to carry it in the car rather than the float). Equine first aid kits are available at good saddlery and tack stores. Ask your vet for advice regarding contents.

**Show kits**

If you are attending shows and events, you will need to put together a show kit, as well as carrying your 'clean' saddle and tack, and regular grooming kit. Include:

- **Shampoo and conditioner (make sure that your selection will not irritate your horse's skin)**
- **Plaiting/braiding kit (rubber bands, waxed cotton and needles, clips)**
- **Mane and tail sprays**
- **Hoof oil and brushes**
- **Tail bandages**
- **Hoods for mane plait protection**
- **Chalk**
- **Vaseline**
- **A clean show rug**
- **A clean show halter**
- **Saddle and tack cleaning kit**

## Let's look at the horse's health, safety and protection

When considering your horse's health, you need to be aware of their normal vital signs and carry out daily routine wellness checks. An equine first aid kit is a must and one should be accessible at the stable/paddock area and within easy reach if you are transporting your horse. For horse vital signs information refer back to the *Entwined* toolkit on the website oceaneasy.net. As mentioned, know where your horse sits in the normal range and record this data and display the information where you and other carers can refer to it quickly should it be required in an emergency.

If your horse becomes sick or injured, you will need to contact your vet immediately. Make sure that you are wearing personal protective equipment—also known as PPE—(disposable gloves, face mask, apron and eye protection) when attending a sick or injured horse to limit cross-infection and the possibility of spreading disease.

Prevention is always better than cure, so ensure:

- **That you have an emergency plan for your horse (include the contact information of your vet)**
- **That you keep your equine first aid kit well stocked**
- **Your horse is vaccinated against disease (ask your vet for preventative vaccines required in your area)**
- **You have a worming programme in place**
- **You groom and wash down your horse regularly**
- **You take preventative measures against biting flies and insects (such as ticks)**
- **Your horse is wearing protective equipment:**
  - **During exercise (boots and bandages)**
  - **In the stable (stable bandages and rugs)**
  - **In the paddock (rugs and fly/insect protection)**
  - **When being transported**

There is an emergency plan template available in the *Entwined* toolkit on the website oceaneasy.net

## Let's look at rider safety and protection

When riding your horse, you should always wear an approved **safety helmet**. You should also wear a safety helmet when handling the horse from the ground: statistics from hospital records show that most accidents involving head injuries happen on the ground around horses! Make sure that your helmet complies with the highest safety standards and if you should suffer a fall and a knock to the head, replace your helmet and dispose of the old helmet after cutting away the chin straps (so that it can't be used again in error). Also be aware that helmets have a shelf life and should be replaced at the manufacturers' recommended intervals.

Wearing **closed footwear** is a must around horses; no matter how good their ground manners, accidents happen! Consider steel toe capped boots for extra protection.

When leading, lunging or riding your horse, **wearing gloves** will offer added grip and can prevent friction burns if your horse should shy on the lead or pull away on the lunge.

**Back protectors** to avoid spinal injuries resulting from a fall are also available and come in various designs and safety ratings. Inflatable jackets to limit bulk and offer cushioning on impact are also popular but do require regular maintenance.

As mentioned, with horse health concerns, make sure you have **personal protective equipment** (PPE) available to use (disposable gloves, face mask, apron or disposable suit and eye protection).

You should also wear PPE if you are using chemicals and sprays as a method of weed control in the paddock.

Make sure that you also protect your skin from over-exposure to the harmful rays of the sun. Use UV-blocking sun sleeves or a long-sleeved shirt made of cotton or **UV-inhibiting material**.

**Eye protection** is important. If you are wearing prescription glasses or sunglasses make sure they are made of shatter-resistant material such as polycarbonate and have UV-inhibiting filters to protect you from the sun's rays. Be mindful that your eyes are part of your body language. If your horse is reading human (you), you may be covering up some cues and signals. This is especially important with young horses or horses that are new to being handled.

# SUMMARY

I hope that within *Entwined* you have seen how the connection between human and horse is interwoven; how understanding not only ourselves but also our horses can be enriching and rewarding.

Preparing for horse ownership or indeed revisiting a relationship with your horse should be an exciting escapade. Planning for their care should be reassuring, actively designing your future together. I hope you become further entwined with the horses in your life.

**Angela**

# END NOTES

The *Entwined* toolkit can be found at oceaneasy.net including—time budget, money budget, stress assessment, dominance, vital signs and emergency plan.

Further information on the human mindset from *Tanja Mitton can be found at tanjamitton.com

Further information on horse behaviour, learning and training from *Georgia Bruce can be found at clickertraining.org

An image library for 'How the Horse's Mind Works' can be found at oceaneasy.net

An image library for "How the Horse's Body Works' can be found at oceaneasy.net

Printed in the United States
By Bookmasters